LIGHTNING
in a
Bottle

LIGHTNING
in a
Bottle

Proven Lessons for
Leading Change

David Baum

DEARBORN™
A **Kaplan Professional** Company

This publication is designed to provide accurate and authoritative information in regard to the subject matter covered. It is sold with the understanding that the publisher is not engaged in rendering legal, accounting, or other professional service. If legal advice or other expert assistance is required, the services of a competent professional should be sought.

Acquisitions Editor: Jean Iversen
Managing Editor: Jack Kiburz
Interior Design: Lucy Jenkins
Cover Design: Scott Rattray, Rattray Design
Typesetting: Elizabeth Pitts

Published by Dearborn, a Kaplan Professional Company

Printed in the United States of America

00 01 02 10 9 8 7 6 5 4 3 2 1

Library of Congress Cataloging-in-Publication Data

Baum, David H.
   Lightning in a bottle : proven lessons for leading change / David Baum.
     p. cm.
   ISBN 0-7931-3595-8
   1. Organizational change. 2. Industrial management. 3. Leadership.
4. Peters, Thomas J.   I. Title.
   HD58.8.B376   2000
   658.4′063—dc21   99-088245

DEDICATION

To my wife Terry
and stepchildren Kate and Galen,
who got me to move to New Hampshire
and really learn about change.

CONTENTS

ACKNOWLEDGMENTS

In writing this book, many voices came into play. The following appreciations are in order.

I extend my most heartfelt thanks to my parents, Bernice and Stanley Baum, who taught me to look hard, question often, and laugh a lot.

To my colleagues, Nancy Aronson, Beverly Arsht, Sandra Janoff, Dick and Emily Axelrod, Chris Cappy, Jim Hassinger, and Pat Sanaghan, for the always-illuminating conversations and breakthroughs in learning.

To my significant teachers of change, Angeles Arrien and Rod Napier, who at various times in my life helped me to understand the connection between theory and real life.

To all those clients who let me practice what I preached. In particular, I want to thank Tom Kalaris and Sandi Schroeder at Barclays Capital; Kim Roffman at Shell Oil; Mary Jane Mastorovich and Jolene Tornabeni at Inova Health Systems; Rick Little and Bill Reese at The International Youth Foundation; Jerry Nunnally at The California Institute of Technology; Sonia Madison at Health Partners; and Jeff Jasnoff at Subaru, Manor Care, and Sunrise Assisted Living. I gained terrific insights when allowed to poke around your organizations. Thank you.

To Ben Perez, for reading the draft and providing a truthful assessment from a hardheaded business perspective—it really lit a fire under me.

To Swift Corwin, for his always helpful support and great chapter titling.

To Karl Weber, my agent and editor, who believed I should write a book, supported me every step of the way, and never once said, "I told you so."

To my editor at Dearborn Trade, Jean Iversen, for her unfailingly straight word and consistent help. It's a far better book—thanks, Jean.

To Barbara, my office assistant, for keeping the home fires burning.

To David and Cynthia Knudsen of Northwaters for modeling what a truly humane and world-class organization looks like.

Finally, I believe no book, let alone a first one, comes without a boatload of inspiration. In no particular order, I am grateful to Morgan Henderson, Ruby, Virginia McKenzie, Pamela Nelson, Julie Roberts, Coleman Barks, Kathy Karn, Elizabeth Murray, Larry Baum, Jellaludin Rumi, Tracy Sarriugarte, Peter and June Lyons, Nancy Feehan, Mo Maxfield, Judy Ostrow, Patrick O'Neill, and Margaret Condon.

INTRODUCTION

Lightning in a Bottle

It is not only for what we do that we are held
responsible, but also for what we do not do.

—Moliere

As a consultant, I have been involved in countless
organizational change efforts, big and small. Some were
for Fortune 50 companies such as Shell Oil or Barclays
Bank, cost up to $100 million and involved thousands of
people. Some were smaller efforts in community-based
not-for-profits, affecting only a handful of individuals.
My travels have taken me into institutions like Wharton
and the California Institute of Technology to teach what
I know to executives and leaders.

I have been on the inside of everything from an $80
million software installation, involving one of the largest
corporations in the world, to a presidential effort headed
by Colin Powell to increase volunteerism among U.S.
citizens. I've been fortunate enough to have worked with
national governments (Northern Ireland), large organizations, tribal communities, and local environmental
groups. I have even traveled two continents with three

circuses as a clown and fire-eater (yes, I know—a small leap).

When it comes to managing change, these organizations have more similarities than differences. Regardless of who's involved, what the change issues are, when it's to happen, and what the benefits will be, change "works" when critical and important principles are maintained. Those in leadership, either intuitively or through a plan, follow certain key, guiding principles that make the change successful and effective. And when these efforts fail (and many do fail) or fall below expectations, it usually is because smart people do stupid things—acting in a manner that runs contrary to any chances for success.

Given that change is a daily part of our lives, it's truly stunning that we are not better trained to deal with change. From the earliest time humans walked the planet, our environment has challenged us to adapt and adjust. Yet with all the lessons from the past that could have been learned, we still have not developed successful strategies for change management. We consistently bumble around. We are still struggling with the concept of graceful change, still out there (sometimes accompanied by a battery of consultants) creating havoc during transitions. In essence, when it comes to efforts to effect organizational change, we are trying to catch lightning in a bottle—hoping providence or sheer good luck will bring us through.

Recently, I was watching my two-year-old nephew trying to build a tower with blocks. With each failure, as the blocks would fall around him, he'd incorporate a refinement into the next version until he created a structure that was stable and to his liking. He learned from his mistakes and self-corrected as he went along. I'll never forget the intensity and commitment he brought to his task as he worked his project.

Unfortunately, most organizations do not have the inherent wisdom of a two-year-old. We do not learn from our mistakes and course-correct when it comes to organizational change. We do the same thing over and over again and somehow expect different results. At best, this is a blueprint for frustration; at worst, it's a path to insanity.

When my consulting colleagues and I get together and talk about why some client's efforts didn't work, our stories are almost always the same. The names and faces are of course different, but the script could be a template of leadership dysfunction, lack of involvement, poor coordination, and ultimately the absence of common sense.

It doesn't have to be that way. *Lightning in a Bottle* distills my experiences into a useable and accessible collection of lessons learned. Some are cutting-edge insights, some are straightforward, even obvious (though often overlooked) principles, and a few may even have a touch of the profound about them; but all are intended to provide you with ideas you can use today, in whatever organizations you're a part of.

At any given time, there are hundreds of books on the market regarding change management—many written by people a lot smarter than me. What is often missing, however, is a format that provides information in a simple and digestible manner. This book attempts to take the reader through a variety of short and concrete concepts that, in my experience, have been instrumental in making a change effort successful.

Turn to any page, read from any spot—if you find something useful, put it into practice. But above all, I encourage you to reflect on your own change-management strategies while reading about the experiences of others. That way, you can find ways to increase your own effectiveness.

The great naturalist and essayist Henry David Thoreau once said, "If you have built castles in the air, your work need not be lost; that is where they should be. Now put the foundations under them." This book contains foundations my clients have found helpful over the years in their change efforts. They represent the growing edge of my work over the years.

As Glendon Johnson, former CEO of John Alden Insurance, once told me, "A cow never stays milked." Likewise, businesses are always changing and growing. I hope the ideas and strategies outlined in this book are as useful to you as they have been to others.

—David Baum

RESISTANCE—
VISIBLE AND INVISIBLE

The only person who likes change is a wet baby.

—Yiddish Proverb

At some basic level, we are all resistant to change. In any organization facing change, the question is not whether there will be resistance but rather how, when, where, and in what ways resistance will manifest itself. Think of it as a law of basic human physics, if you will. Change implies movement, and movement always has some level of resistance associated with it.

I am never amazed at the human capacity to be creative in conflict and resistance. While terribly frustrating, we can come up with stunningly brilliant ways to sabotage, either overtly or covertly, change efforts.

Part of the problem in managing resistance is the sense of shock or even betrayal we feel if those we work with are not fully engaged. But if we understand that resistance is a natural emotion that springs from almost any change, then it is easier to move to a place of neutrality without judgment and to manage the resistance more effectively.

Try to anticipate and proactively address the resistance that will emerge. Your goal is to deflate any unspoken tensions that may exist around change. This can be tricky—you don't want to create a self-fulfilling prophecy. Use your judgment, but do speak up regarding the fears and other emotions you suspect are simmering below the surface. Give voice to what you believe has been unspoken.

This helps in two ways. First, the unspoken resistance is always much more powerful than the spoken resistance. Consider for a moment a time when you had an opportunity to talk about something that upset you. Didn't talking help to relieve the pressure cooker of internal tension? Second, by unveiling a hidden issue, you open the door to dialogue and greater participation. You allow the opportunity for yourself and others to understand the fear and empathize with those who feel it. A leader who appears to understand is a leader others will follow, regardless of their resistance.

Bring resistance out into the open where it can be dealt with honestly and fairly rather than left to fester—and ultimately explode. Giving voice to "what is" is a very helpful strategy.

THE MYTH OF
THE GOLDEN RULE

When a cell in your body begins to be
self-centered, taking only in regard to
its own needs and ignoring those of
its neighbor, we call it *cancer.*

—Ra Bonawitz

Remember the golden rule, "Do unto others as you would have them do unto you"? It's a lovely adage, which most of us learned early on and probably teach our kids—a phrase many of us value as a life lesson.

Unfortunately, there's a big problem with applying the golden rule to organizational issues—a very big problem.

The golden rule assumes that the way I like to be treated will be the same way you like to be treated. That is the basic philosophical underpinning of "Do unto others." When applied specifically to organizational problem solving, it assumes that my approach to conflict mediation, decision making, and information gathering will be the same as yours.

Many of us have built a personal life strategy around this assumption since we were children. It's how we've dealt with the world. It is a style of survival that is old and revered.

But as a strategy, it has a critical flaw: It is terribly ego-centric. It assumes that the way I see the world is the same way you see the world. Thus, my way is the primary way, the right way, the correct way. It's a logical conclusion, if you were raised with the golden rule. However, if you shift your thinking to a different viewpoint, you will open possibilities for potential success that were unavailable before.

Our slant on the world often doesn't allow us to see the humor or absurdity of our own perspectives. This narrowness impacts the decisions and actions we take to effectively negotiate the differences that usually arise during change.

It's important to realize the simple axiom that no one sees the world in exactly the same way you do. Assuming the golden rule can be inherently dangerous in matters ranging from communication to conflict and negotiation to decision making. This is especially true if implicitly held beliefs and values are enacted without the benefit of setting the context of your thinking.

To be truly effective you must have the capacity to understand, and at times, apply viewpoints other than your own. It requires a new version of the golden rule: "Do unto others *the way they want to be done unto.*" It's a small philosophical shift that can make a world of difference.

THE REALITIES WE CREATE

The last of human freedoms is to choose one's attitude in any given moment.

—Victor Frankl

Quickly now, what does this say?

OPPORTUNITYISNOWHERE

If you're like most people, you responded with "Opportunity is nowhere." Fair answer. In fact, about 85 percent of all readers will give that reply.

But let's try it again. Now what does it say?

OPPORTUNITY IS NOW HERE

Now you see a sentence with a very different implication. It's all a matter of perception.

Perception is our internal response to or interpretation of information presented to us. It profoundly shapes our response to change. Perception is a key element in any endeavor involving a changing environment. Often it is both the cause and the effect of what happens in a change process.

Like snowflakes, no two individuals' perceptions of any situation are exactly alike. How we perceive reality is a very personal matter. But our perceptions, though individually very different, can be shaped and changed to provide us with a more effective view of the world. By following a simple formula, we can alter the way we perceive life's events. This is an important shift toward managing changes more gracefully and with less negative impact. When you positively change the way you see events, you automatically improve your outlook in general.

It's essential to remember that how we perceive reality dictates how we respond to it. Manage the internal realities and you manage a lot.

THE ABCs OF PERCEPTION

Circumstance has no power over you.
Your inner weather is always and
forever at your command.

—Olga Rosmanith

For every change that occurs in our world, a simple formula can be followed that allows us to better understand the choices we make regarding our perception of that situation. It is based on the famous maxim of the French philosopher René Descartes: "I think, therefore I am," with its crucial implication—we create our own realities. I call this formula the ABCs. In any time of change, whether you're moving to a new job, switching software systems, or going through a corporate restructuring, the three steps we label "A," "B," and "C" will always occur.

"A" stands for activating event. The activating event is the experience itself. It's what happens to you, the action that starts in motion your thoughts and reactions.

"A" represents all the things that can occur on a daily basis. Essentially, it's life itself. Suppose, for instance, that late one night you hear a noise downstairs. The activating event in this case is the noise. It wakes you up and starts you thinking. It's what initiates the process.

"B" stands for your belief system regarding the event. Our belief system springs into action inside our brains when we start thinking about what the activating event means to us. These internal machinations sometimes create an altogether different picture from the event itself, because of all the old messages, lessons, and fears of your lives that, if triggered by the right activating event, can come boiling to the surface quickly. When you hear a noise at night, your belief system may trigger fear, perhaps convincing you that there's a burglar in the house: "My God, I'm being robbed. I've got to protect my kids!" This leads to the final step . . .

"C," which stands for the consequence that arises from your belief system. This is the natural outflowing of the way we think—the behavior we choose based on the beliefs we have about the world in general and the activating event in particular. Essentially, it is our response—our "reaction"—to the situation itself.

I have a friend whose reaction one night, based on the belief that her home was threatened by a burglar, was to call the police and herd her children up on the roof. Mind you, this was at 3:00 A.M. during a frigid winter in upstate New York. Imagine her feelings when the police discovered that the vicious threat to society responsible for the nocturnal alarm was the family hamster (who I understand is now serving life behind bars). I'm amazed my friend had the guts to tell this story later.

Of course, everyone's belief system is very different. Our unique individual experiences shape how we look at the world. The key is to understand that the ways in which we internalize external changes in our lives impact the ways in which we manage those changes. If you can't affect the external events of change, then focus on the internal turbulence of your perceptions. Ultimately, this is the only thing over which you have complete control.

How many changes have you seen where people's imaginations went wild? How many events have you been a part of where the picture in your head bore little relation to reality? Our internal movie screen drives us, nothing else. Get that and you're in control to a greater level during change than you ever thought possible.

Here's an example: Three people spend a night on a mountain. The next morning, they compare their experiences. The first person says, "It was great! The moon was up. The small night animals of the forest were all around me. I heard the romantic cry of a loon. It was fantastic."

The second person says, "It was horrible. The moon lit up the woods so I couldn't get a wink of sleep. Large animals were roaming all around me, and to make matters worse, I heard a wolf howling and I swear it sounded hungry!"

The third person says, "No big deal. I went to sleep. I woke up. End of story."

Same night, same woods, three very different experiences, based upon different belief systems.

To a large extent, we can't change life. It just is. Life is filled with struggle, change, and surprise. If it weren't, they would have given it another name. Organizational changes, personal conflicts, missed flights, unfortunate accidents, and other unexpected things happen. We try, but often we can't change these events. At best, we may only be able to influence them.

Thankfully, we have greater influence over our internal views. It's how we perceive these events and frame them into a belief system that determines whether we feel in control or not. If you can more gracefully accept what *is* as opposed to what you think *should be,* your sense of reality will shift, producing a greater feeling of acceptance and commitment. And by changing our beliefs, the consequences can often be radically different.

It's the difference between Lee Iaccoca, the much-admired auto executive who played a key role in saving Chrysler, and a thousand other managers you never heard

of. The consequence of a personal and business "failure"—being fired from his job at General Motors—was
different for Iacocca than it would be for most executives,
because his belief system surrounding the activating event
was different. Trite as it may sound, Iaccoca chose to see
failure as an opportunity. Our beliefs drive results, not the
random tumbling of life's activating changes.

I love what Jack Nicklaus, arguably the greatest golfer
of all time, once said: "I may lose, but I'm never beaten."
Change the way in which you view an event and you can
change the consequences of the event itself.

FIGHT OR FLIGHT—
FORMS OF RESISTANCE

When one door closes, another opens.
But we often look so long and so regretfully
at the closed door that we do not notice
the one which has opened for us.

—Helen Keller

Peter Drucker, the revered scholar of management,
once said, "Employees are infinite in their abilities to come
up with creative ways of sabotaging the efforts of their
bosses." Remembering that all change brings resistance,

you can expect that your staff will be infinite in their abilities to develop creative strategies for impeding change.

However, it helps to know that, from the myriad possibilities available, humans essentially respond in one of only two ways. Resistance comes bearing one of two possible forms: fight or flight.

The *fight* response can be broken into two categories: active aggression and passive aggression. During active aggression, our heart beats faster, our adrenaline flows, and our pupils dilate. You will hear comments like, "What kind of a company is this? The quality of service is going right down the toilet. We used to be a family in this organization." People will get visibly upset and angry, rising to the height of their emotions.

The image is one of a warrior going into battle, with weapons drawn and energy rushing forward in anticipation of the impending clash. But the battles we're referring to here will occur at water fountains, in elevators, in company meetings large and small. Often, those engaged in active aggression are branded as "difficult employees." However, be aware that this behavior is just one form of fight resistance.

The other form of fight is passive aggression. This is often the resistance strategy of those who are not in a position of power. Those engaged in passive aggression get sullen and quiet; their eyes become glazed, like those of deer in the headlights. You can see this look at almost every department meeting you go to where the organization is announcing some type of change.

The script is almost predictable. The leaders will finish making their case for change, and the head honcho will then say something like, "Well, that concludes our presentation. Are there any questions or reactions?" There will be a long and painful silence followed by, "No? Terrific. I know I can count on your support."

But the rank-and-file employees then leave the room, get in the elevator, and begin to say things like, "That's the stupidest thing I have ever heard." That is the passive aggressive response to change. It is a subtle form of the fight response, one that moves underground rather than in the open. It tends to rear its head in smaller groupings, in quieter tones, but these qualities only make it more insidious and difficult to manage.

The second major form of resistance is *flight*. This behavior is an active, literal form of withdrawal. Individuals engaged in flight either leave or go into total denial that the change is occurring. The impulse is for no engagement in the process. During any major change process, it is not uncommon for many employees to have their résumés on the street or at least be talking with their peers about doing so. Flight is actually a more difficult form of resistance to manage than fight, because the issues are often unseen or flatly denied. Finding the root causes as they emerge can be a taxing and difficult process.

Part of the problem is that we will always identify the active form of fight behavior as resistant without giving too much attention to the less aggressive, passive fight-or-flight form of resistance. This is a mistake. Attention needs to be equally placed so that all forms of resistance are managed. I have seen many organizations where major change initiatives went by the boards because too little attention was paid to the quieter voices; so much effort went to the squeaky wheels that the subtler forms of resistance went unnoticed.

Some forms of flight look like promises made and then not kept. Others include an even more subtle form of sabotage—doing exactly what is asked, to the letter! The problem is, of course, that all substantial change efforts require some form of course-correction. Like tacking with a sailboat, an organization in the throes of change is engaged in a constant reevaluation of effort, which requires some type of self-managed initiative. But if employees refuse to engage, the necessary adjustments will never be made. When the change effort goes belly-up, the flight-prone resister will innocently say, "Don't look at me. I did exactly what you asked me to."

As an organizational leader, you need to watch for all forms of resistance and manage accordingly. Don't get caught listening only to the voice that is the loudest. Seek out the quieter voices. Engage those who may have been around the organization a long time, and may seem to blend into the woodwork. Assume that every individual may have concerns that can lead him or her to act in a way that undermines the change effort. This is not paranoia, but an understanding of the more subtle elements of resistance.

THE FUELING FORCES BEHIND RESISTANCE

The future is that time when you'll wish you'd done what you aren't doing now.

—Unknown

When we are resistant to change, it is usually based on one of three fueling forces.

The first fueling force is fear of the unknown. It's a huge anxiety that can fuel enormous passions. Picture it this way: We are in some ways like birds in a cage whose door is always open. We can fly away any time, yet many of us choose instead to spend our days rocking back and forth on a swinging perch, comfortable in a place that we know well. For just one example, how many people do you know right now who are desperately unhappy in their marriages yet choose to stay married because of their fear of what it would be like to be single?

The need to know is very strong in human nature, and we rebel against events that cause us to face an unknown future. We are reluctant to take what Antonio Machado, the great Spanish poet, once called "that first, fierce step into the unknown without any thought of return."

The second fueling force behind resistance to change is our desire for a predictable external environment. As massive change affects how we work and how we function, we lose our ability to predict the outcome of things we do. This issue is heavily tied into the feeling of trust. When you can predict an outcome, you are more likely to trust it. That is why, for example, during the civil rights struggles of the 1960s, African-Americans from the southern states often said that they trusted southern bigots more than northern liberals. At least they could *predict* southern behavior.

With loss of predictability, our trust level drops, and as this happens, our resistance goes up.

The third force is the discomfort we have in breaking old work patterns, habits, and norms. We humans by nature are very routinized, driven by instinct to create hundreds of daily rituals. That's how we deal and cope with the world. We sleep on the same side of the bed every night, shower and dress the same way every morning, and drive to work following the same route every day. And at work, we often communicate, process information, and make decisions in the same, ritualized, routinized ways.

The problem with these rituals is that they only work so far. When our world is in flux, our routine patterns become less effective in managing life. As that happens, our anxieties go up.

To use a metaphor, we are sometimes like small fish called remoras that attach themselves to sharks for the benefit of both. The truth is, we can't control the outside world any more than a remora can control the shark it's attached to. The secret is not to achieve total control or predictability but rather to get comfortable with the direction you're going and enjoy the ride. After all, the remora never forgets it's the remora and not the shark. To believe otherwise is setting yourself up for huge disappointment.

In Yiddish, they say, *Menschen tracht. Un got lacht.* Translation: "Man plans. Then God laughs."

When we are asked to change, we ask ourselves two questions at an unconscious gut level. About 30 percent of the time, we ask, "Can I do it?" That is, do I have the skills, aptitude, training, and resources to pull off what's expected of me? And we hope the answer is yes. If you are in position of leadership, it is your responsibility to make sure that your people have what they need to do the job. If they don't, it is cruel and unusual punishment to ask them to do it.

The other 70 percent of the time, people faced with the need to change ask, "Do I want to do it?" That is, when I weigh the pain against the gain, is what I will get more valuable than what I must give?

I was involved in a consulting engagement recently where a sophisticated software system was being installed in a Fortune 50 company. We found that those two simple questions, "Can I do it?" and "Do I want to do it?" could be used to guide the foundation of a massive change implementation effort. Every meeting we held with the company's senior leadership started with a genuine dialogue about whether the employees had the capability to change and whether they would really benefit from changing. The support systems of training and communication we subsequently developed were driven by the repeated asking of these two questions.

THE ONLY REAL INTEREST IS SELF-INTEREST

If you didn't get all the things you wanted,
you can still be grateful for all the things
you didn't want that you didn't get.

—Unknown

Ultimately, your employees do not work for you, the department, the organization, the board of directors, or even your company's customers or clients. They work for themselves.

As we've already suggested, in a time of organizational change, one of leadership's responsibilities is to help employees see the benefits of change. But beware! What matters isn't the benefit in your eyes, or the eyes of the board, or even the eyes of the customers you serve. All that really matters is the individual benefits that each employee sees for his or her own life.

Many company change efforts founder because leaders misunderstand this truth. A major mistake commonly observed is the "selling" of benefits on a scale larger than the personal needs of the individual. To discuss larger issues of change—how much better the company will run once the change is implemented, for example, or the wonderful increases in profitability that the organization will enjoy—without addressing the private, personal needs of your audience is an exercise in futility.

The truth is that the only real interest is self-interest. It's not that humans are inherently selfish, but rather that all change is essentially local. Thus, if you want to change an organization, the battle for hearts and minds must be fought on the field of personal value. Employees must perceive that they have a strong personal stake in change. Remember, people will always do what you want them to do if what you want them to do is what they want to do. The question is, do you know what they want to do? Are you close enough to the people who work for you to effectively articulate what will motivate them? If not, you'd better get to work.

Finally, remember this. During times of large-scale change, there is often a moment when each individual must choose between self-interest and the common good. Many change efforts have failed at that moment. But the most effective change processes are those where there is no such choice—where the change can honestly be framed as consistent with both self-interest and the interests of the organization as a whole. Where there is real benefit for the organization *and* the individual, resistance will be less acute and more manageable.

Focus your attention as a leader on these areas where change offers benefits to everyone involved. This is where you will enjoy the maximum impact. Your efforts here can open a wedge that will help produce broader changes across the board.

THE BENEFITS OF NOT CHANGING

Ours is a world where people don't know
what they want and are willing to go
through hell to get it.

—Don Marquis

There's a joke my grandmother used to tell. "In the old country, we had a cousin who thought he was a chicken. He acted like a chicken in every way, clucking, crowing, scratching. We would have taken him to a psychiatrist to be cured . . . but we needed the eggs!"

Often when individuals refuse to change, the reason is that they derive benefits from *not* changing. Even if the benefit is small—like the comfort of facing a known situation rather than an unknown one—there is a value. If none existed, we'd change immediately!

Years ago as a graduate student, I had a client in counseling who weighed 390 pounds. John had been on every diet known to man—Pritikin, Weight Watchers, Jenny Craig, Nutri Systems, OptiFast, the Bahamian diet—you name it, he'd tried it. On every diet, he would lose between 30 and 50 pounds and, then, with uncanny predictability, would bounce back to his previous weight.

A part of every program was for John to receive counseling on the benefits of weight loss. He knew them all: health, longevity, self-esteem—he could list the benefits at the drop of a hat. What his counselors never explored was the benefits John derived from not changing his behavior—from weighing 390 pounds! But until we did so, he was doomed to stay on the perpetual weight-loss roller coaster.

What, you may be thinking, could possibly be the benefits in weighing 390 pounds? The answer was very interesting. First, there were the work expectations. They were low. While everyone else at his company was on overdrive, John was on cruise control. The typical comment from John's supervisors and colleagues was, "John's got enough trouble in his life, he doesn't need any more." So the company colluded with John's poor work ethic by protecting him, and he was subtly rewarded at work for his weight problem.

The second benefit was John's sex life, or lack thereof. Whenever he was bold enough to pursue an attraction into an attempt at a relationship, he would inevitably get turned down. Then he would say to himself, "She's not rejecting me, she's rejecting my weight!" This comforting excuse for his romantic failure became a very powerful defense against John's intimacy fears.

Finally came the kicker. One great universal truth in life is this: If you're not getting any respect in your job, and no love in your personal life, who is the one and only person you can turn to, no matter what? It's the same person the world over: your mother!

In John's case, Mama was from Italy, stood five foot two, dressed in perpetual black (her husband had died 18 years earlier and she was in mourning), and wore orthopedic shoes. As family custom dictated, John would visit Mama once a week, every Sunday. She would open her door, stare him in the eye, and say, "Gianni, you're looking thin!" Then she would feed him with three meat courses, two soups, four fish courses, three kinds of pasta, two desserts, and four kinds of bread. Would she cook enough for two? Of course not! She'd cook enough for 20. And the leftovers? She'd send John home at the end of the day with two huge shopping bags filled with food. John would then spend the rest of the week literally filling himself up on all the love and personal support he was getting nowhere else in his life.

John and I spent days talking through these realities behind his weight problem. When he realized the benefits he was getting from his size, the pounds rolled off him like water. In two years, John got down to 185 pounds.

He looked fabulous. The crowning moment came when he turned all his old suits over to a used clothing store for large men. As he was leaving the store, he passed someone of his former weight. It was, John said, "As if I was passing my former life." He never would have been able to change his food behavior had he not come to understand the complex dynamics of not changing.

Most change efforts in organizations are focused on the benefits to change. Rarely is any attention paid to the benefits individuals or organizations get from not changing. But if one does not change despite the clear benefits, the reason is obvious. At an underlying level, there are bigger benefits to not changing.

For the leader, this implies two actions. First, spend time working with key individuals to understand the full dynamics of the change effort. Don't shy away from the difficult question of the value in not changing. You may be afraid to ask about it because you think that raising the issue will reinforce the resistance. It's not true. Just because you don't ask doesn't mean your employees don't have strong feelings. The silence just prevents you from understanding the issues and reacting accordingly.

Second, you need to help your employees understand that not to change will be, in the long run, more painful than to change. Often the deepest fear is of job loss. Yet, in a sense, this is not a real issue. During most large-scale organizational changes, every employee has already lost his old job. The only question is: What will the new job look like? This must be answered honestly and directly.

I love what scientist Stephen Hawking says: "The one question you can never ask is, 'Do I want to change?' You can only ask, 'To what will I change and how will I do it?'"

TRUST AND CONTROL

**Do not pray for dreams equal to your powers.
Pray for powers equal to your dreams.**

—Philip Brooks

There is a simple yet unspoken equation underlying much of human life:

Behavior = Need

Resistance, however it manifests itself, is just one form of human behavior. Thus, the equation we've presented can help to explain it. Whether it takes the form of fight or flight, anger or passivity, all resistance is just an outward symptom of an underlying need.

Now, when you ask people, "What is the benefit you get from resisting change?" the most common response, based on the primary need most people have, is the desire to retain control. Think about all the various strategies you or others may have used to resist change. Procrastination, angrily fighting back, asking a thousand testing questions—whatever the behavior, the underlying need is for control. If you probe for the thinking behind the behavior, you may hear comments like, "I wanted to delay things as much as possible," "I was hoping that I could get things to go my way," or "I wanted to prove my view was the right one so I could get what I wanted." Essentially, the underlying desire is for more control of the situation.

Because behavior and need are two sides of the same equation, what happens with one affects the other. Imagine a seesaw, with the resistance behavior on one side and the underlying need on the other. As one goes up, the other goes down.

Because most organizations provide their employees with very little control during change efforts, the resultant levels of resistance will be high. A key strategy to managing obstruction then becomes obvious: *to decrease resistance, increase control.*

So as the change leader, you need to ask both for yourself and for others, "In what ways can I provide more control?" Control takes many forms. It often looks like information, input, solicitation of views, and consideration of perspective. That's why creating forums and processes that give people a base level of control, and with it a sense of safety, are critical to managing anxiety and resistant behaviors.

In nine out of ten organizations I get called into where resistance is high, there's diminished control on the part of those affected. It's almost inevitable; after all, in most business environments, the dynamics of the organization are set up to centralize control in a very small group. This, of course, also sets up a strong potential for high resistance:

Low control = High resistance

Trust and control are two sides of the same coin. Where an organization does not trust is where it will inevitably try to control. That is why many large-scale reorganizations are conducted in a vacuum, often planned at retreats or closed-door meetings by those with traditional power, perhaps assisted by outside consultants with no connections among the rank-and-file employees of the organization. The inevitable result is diminished trust levels throughout and a spiral of resistance that is tough to break.

The spiral works something like this: Leadership often doesn't trust those impacted by change to move in the right direction (after all, that's why *we're* the leaders). This low trust level means the leaders give little control to those below them. With little control, those impacted feel a greater level of resistance. As they act on their resistance, leadership says, "See. We told you those people couldn't be trusted. The only solution is to clamp down." The level of trust drops even further, and the negative spiral accelerates.

Where it all starts is of little consequence. The key is to break the spiral with a significant action that will disrupt the pattern of mistrust and resistance. To find a way to do this, always ask yourself two crucial questions: "Where can I provide more control to those personally affected by change?" and "What are the areas where I do not trust them?"

Be honest on this last one. It raises the mirror close. Uncomfortable? You bet. But the truth needs to be faced.

THE FOUR STAGES
OF COMMITMENT

Eighty percent of success is showing up.

—Woody Allen

When asked to change, people rarely jump headfirst into the pool shouting, "Great! What took you so long?" No matter what value a change will bring, it is unrealistic to assume that employees will walk forward committed on Day One to implementation.

Rather, the process for most people is to slowly dip their toes into the water and ease into the shallow end, splashing a little water around and complaining about how cold it is. For most people, commitment to the "new way" goes in emotional stages, with each stage having certain requirements and prerequisites. How those stages are managed and modeled helps determine whether your people move forward to a quick transition or stop and floun-der in the process. And understanding that commitment doesn't happen overnight can be helpful in and of itself.

The four stages of transition are denial, resistance, exploration, and commitment. These will be discussed in detail in the following pages. We move through these psychologically with deliberate pacing, and we do not skip any stage.

As we've already seen, what most people want during any transition is a sense of control—the feeling that they can impact the direction they are taking. So as one naturally moves through the four stages of commitment, the more control (and thus safety) one feels, the quicker one will transition to the next stage. Thus, the more control your employees have, the easier it is for them to move toward the final stage of full commitment.

Yet most of us want everyone to jump ahead and go right to commitment. We expect our employees to jump from denial to commitment with just a little pep talk. But each stage is a prerequisite for movement to the next. That is just the way the mind works. Even those of us who are willing to jump headfirst into the pool will go through a shortened version of this process.

STAGE 1:
GETTING BEYOND DENIAL

If you can't find the truth right where you are,
where else do you think you will find it?

—Jack Kornfield

Have you ever been in a situation—at work, maybe, or in your family life—where you knew something was different, but you didn't quite know what it was? There was this little voice inside that kept nagging at you—an instinctual voice that kept tugging at your shirttails, whispering, "Look up." Yet somehow you didn't—couldn't— look up.

This is what denial feels like. It is a state of mind in which we choose to ignore the information around us, regardless of its importance. Denial can be very powerful, and humans can be very good at it: consider everything from the world's reaction to the Holocaust to the ways a spouse may ignore the clues that his marriage is dissolving. The flight from reality to the short-term comfort of denial is an old and deep human pattern.

During organizational change, denial will speak in many voices. You will hear phrases like, "Everything's fine," "This is no big deal," "I don't want to talk about it," "I will find a way around it," and, of course, mostly you will hear silence.

There will be avoidance of the topic of change, a sense of going through the motions, and a general pretending that nothing is really happening. It is the Sergeant Schultz approach from television's *Hogan's Heroes:* "I know nothing. I see nothing. I hear nothing."

Surprisingly, when an organization is in the stage of denial, sometimes productivity will actually increase, as if in the belief that if only we work a little harder the need to change will go away. But when we are talking about tidal waves of change, not ripples, doing the same work slightly more diligently is not what's needed.

To move out of denial, it is important to realize that it is essentially a *cognitive* experience—that is, an experience centered on knowledge and understanding. What your employees need first is information as to why the change is occurring. What is the rationale for the change effort? What is it, what will it do, and why are we making the change?

As the leader, your strategy must be to provide information to help your employees understand what the change will mean. The sooner they start to deal with the real issues, the sooner they will move from denial to acceptance and then to action.

Remember that because they are in denial, your message will need to be repeated frequently. John Kotter and Jim Heskitt of Harvard University found that during organizational change, management usually undercommunicates the vision by a factor of ten! So consider what you should say and how often you should say it, and multiply your efforts many times over.

It is also important to be completely honest and clear in describing the benefits and drawbacks of the change. If you don't have all the answers, it's all right to say, "I don't know, but I'll find out and get back to you," or even better, "I don't know. But let's figure it out together." This shifts the locus of control and responsibility back to all your people and helps create ownership and a shared effort in the change.

By providing information frequently and in depth, you also help control the rumor mill that will surely kick in when you start the change effort. Rumors arise because of what I like to call the Blank Space phenomenon: When a blank space occurs, the mind will inevitably fill it in.

Because information is control, wherever there is a gap in information, employees will fill in the gap with their own ideas. A feeling of "knowing" is then created, which helps give a greater sense of control. Real or unreal, these information fillers become reality, and the rumor mill is off and running. And when trust levels are low, individuals will fill the blank space in, not with the best-case scenario, but with the worst-case scenario.

By providing real information, you shrink the gaps into which your employees can project their fears and anxieties. This minimizes the rumors, provides people with a sense of control based in reality, and ultimately makes your job much easier.

As my colleague Pat Sanaghan says, "Whether you like it or not, you are in the communication business." When change is in the offing, this imperative is redoubled.

STAGE 2: RESISTANCE

I was going to buy a copy of *The Power of Positive Thinking,* but then I thought, "What the hell good would that do?"

—Ronnie Shakes

The next stage that one moves to after denial is the stage of active response called *resistance*. If denial is a cognitive and essentially passive experience, then resistance is an emotional and active one.

As leaders, we get upset when resistance occurs. Our feeling is, "Hey, I explained the changes, why are we repeating them and the rationale over and over again? And *now* you're upset?" The unfortunate reality is, after the stage of denial, after our people understand the picture of change and the reasons it's necessary, they then get emotional.

Why? Because of this very simple but profound concept: *All change involves loss.* And all loss evokes strong emotion—ask anyone who's lived through a divorce, a bankruptcy, or a death in the family. This stage of the transition is about *affect*—that is, about emotional reactions. It's about mourning and letting go and struggling with fears and anxieties. You'll hear complaining, gossip, lots of challenging questions, and negativism. You may see mistakes on the job, accidents, careless or sloppy work, and expressions of anger. The short-term gains in productivity that you may have experienced during the denial stage are now long gone. Morale drops like a rock.

How can you cope with this difficult transitional stage? Your primary strategy should be to acknowledge the loss and how your staff is feeling about it. The goal is to allow people to express their feelings, and in so doing move beyond them. But it's crucial to understand the difference between the two phrases, "I understand" and "I agree." "I understand" acknowledges the feeling without justifying the rumors, untruths, or accusations it evokes, while "I agree" colludes with the resistance.

Your job is to listen in a thoughtful and caring manner and allow the emotions to move forward without supporting the arguments they engender. That is the key: You support the process, but not the content of the emotional complaining.

It's vital to listen, and listen hard. Don't argue. If you feel misunderstood, ask people to repeat what they thought you said. This can save a lot of explaining down the road. Accept all feelings—good or bad—as real and honest expressions of other people's issues and concerns.

And remember that feelings change, often even if nothing is done. That is one of the great constants of life.

The deepest struggle, however, may be internal, not external—within your own mind and heart. As a leader, you may be caught in the middle yourself. You may be asked to carry forward a message and actions into which you had no input. You may have your own mixed feelings about the change or the demands it is placing on your time, your energy, your values. My recommendation? Be vigilant in observing your own internal struggles so they don't unconsciously support the resistance. Your staff will watch you like a hawk. The cues they take will come from what they see or don't see. Remember that and act accordingly. Like it or not, your primary responsibility is to amplify the message every chance you get, not filter it. To do this, you need to monitor yourself with rigorous honesty.

You may be tempted to collude with your staff's resistance; to reveal, through a wink, a certain sarcastic tone of voice, an occasional joke or complaint, that you, too, wish there was no need to change your ways or the ways of the organization. Think twice. The truth is, by colluding to support the resistance, you are only making your job more difficult in the long run. It is a short-term gain leading to a long-term struggle.

The "how long" question often comes up. How much time does it take for an individual or a group to move through the stage of resistance? It's a difficult question, and the answer at best is a guess. But, in my experience, if you create opportunities for input and listen without supporting the argument, you can anticipate two to six months of struggling through this stage. It can be a long six months. But if you don't expect an overnight attitude change, knowing that the resistance can and will pass is helpful.

Not everyone in your group will react the same, of course. If your change process is like most, about 15 percent of your folks are going to be thrilled and will only want to know what took you so long. About 15 percent will utterly reject the need to change, and won't be happy no matter what you do. The remaining 70 percent will sit on the fence and quietly watch to see who's winning.

This middle 70 percent is where you need to put most of your time and energy. That is where the victories really count. The 15 percent who are positively excited will need very little support and encouragement. They are already motivated by the change. For the negative 15 percent, there may be nothing you can do. They need to be given a clear message: The train is in the station. You have two options: you can jump on board—in which case, you're welcome—or you will be left standing at the platform as the train pulls out.

There may be little else you can say. The hard truth is, there are some people who will never get beyond the stage of resistance. Make their choices clear and act accordingly. This may be one of the most important responsibilities of leadership. It's certainly one of the hardest.

STAGE 3: EXPLORATION

In times of change, learners inherit the
earth, while the learned find themselves
beautifully equipped to deal with a
world that no longer exists.

—Eric Hoffer

When it comes to change transition, I want to let you know that hope does exist. If you can manage your peoples' anxieties—and perhaps more important, your own—then the next stage that you and they will move to is the stage of exploration. During this stage, you may see confusion as your employees struggle with the process of change, but you will also witness risk-taking and people trying out new things. You will hear positive, optimistic comments like, "This might work after all," "I've got an idea," and "Let's try it another way." The exploration stage is about the birth of hope.

Your strategy is to facilitate this progress so that hope and a sense of meaningful change develop and spread. Every change and the flux it brings provides opportunity for growth and innovation. You need to focus on the positive changes your staff are making and foster an environment that encourages discovery and investigation. This is a time for trial and error, and it is critical to enjoy every victory—even the small ones—and celebrate the successes your team experiences in real and appropriate ways. It is the "new" behaviors and actions, and the successes that come from them, that will truly impact the belief in the future.

It's important to know that change in the middle often looks like failure. Imagine, for instance, that your people are crossing a wide stream. With each step, the water continues to get higher and higher. When the water gets to their chest, what will they instinctively want to do? Turn around and walk back to where they came from! Your responsibility, whether psychologically in the water with them or on the distant shore, is to maintain the vision. When those around you feel the natural frustration that comes from being in that "betwixt and between" place, you need to keep positive movement happening in any way you can.

This is essential because when we get scared, we tend to revert to those behaviors that made us successful in the past. The tendency will almost always be to want to turn around midstream and head back to the side from which we started. Yet paradoxically those habits, patterns, and ways of working will not be the ones required for future growth. The successful style in which you conducted business in the past may be the exact same pattern that will cause you to fail in the future (how many of you even *own* a slide rule?).

When fear takes hold, and people try—unsuccessfully—to revert to old dynamics and systems, the look of frustration and confusion will be evident in their eyes.

How you support them then will be essential to moving the ownership of change to a new level. Resist the temptation of "I told you so" and focus on the gains rather than the losses. Change is rarely straightforward. It is a dance of forward and backward steps. Your responsibility is to provide, in Peter Drucker's words, "The story of where we are going."

Can you consistently paint an honest and compelling picture of the future? It must be something that others are willing to move toward, and that holds value and benefit for them. Create a sense of believability in your employees to make it happen, and happen well. As an engineer going through a major software change once said, "It didn't matter if I thought I could do it. It mattered if my boss thought I could do it." In your organization, be the leader whose belief makes possible the faith of those around you.

STAGE 4: COMMITMENT

There is always one unexpected little moment in life when a door opens to let the future in.

—Graham Greene

Consider this fact. Prior to A.D. 1850—thousands of years after humans first appeared on the earth, and centuries after the earliest stirrings of technology—no human being had ever traveled faster on land than eight miles per hour. Why not?

There are many reasons, but three are most crucial. First, we didn't think it was important to travel faster than eight miles per hour. Second, we didn't see the benefit of traveling faster than eight miles per hour. And third, we didn't think we *could* travel faster than eight miles per hour.

As a leader, to move your organization forward into a new committed place, you need to focus on why the change is occurring, what benefits it will bring, and how your organization can deal with the change.

The English word *commitment* comes from the Latin *commitate,* which means "to keep safe." When we move ourselves and others into commitment, we are keeping safe the vision, purposes, and goals of our future. True commitment does just that.

It keeps all the aspirations and organizational dreams safe so that they can be brought to life in a better future for everyone.

Your primary strategy during the commitment stage should be to first recognize and then reward success when you see it.

Recognition is the first key. Recognizing success is essential so that others can learn from the experience and incorporate those learnings into the next change that comes. If I know success when I see it, then the next time it will be easier to recognize it. Remember when you were first learning to drive? There was so much going on both internally and externally. For instance, you and another car might pull up to opposing stop signs at almost the same time. Who goes first? You'd start, then stop, and then maybe start again until your parent said, "It's fine. Go ahead." After you had acted, your parent might say, "Nice job. That wasn't so bad. Remember, the next time this happens."

Now, as an adult, you don't even give it a second thought. You quickly assess who got there first, the other driver, how aggressive or in a rush he or she seems compared to you, and act accordingly. It is an ongoing process of learning that only comes from experience and doing. Your parent, who provided ongoing guidance regarding successes and mistakes, initially started that learning cycle. As a leader, you must do the same thing. When victories are acknowledged, a capacity for change is built that breeds commitment.

The second key is to reward what you are trying to create. Our employees will watch who and what is rewarded very closely. If the rewards for change—financial and otherwise—are real, then the commitments will be strong and lasting. But if the rewards do not match what you are trying to do, you are in for a very long struggle.

The CEO of one financial organization I work with consistently calls for a greater sense of team spirit and awareness of one department's impact on another. He is tired of decisions being made that help one area but are detrimental to another. Unfortunately, he's in for a long battle, because no matter how loudly he lauds the value of collaboration, the compensation system is set up to reward individual and departmental success. People are paid on individual and departmental bonuses—that is the bottom line! It is also his choice (we've discussed this one at length). When push comes to shove, people will act in their own best self-interests. In all likelihood, he will never achieve the future he wants because he will not reconcile the difference between the desired future and what the organization rewards in the present.

Take a good, hard look at your organization and examine the rewards and recognition programs you've devised. If they don't match what you say you want to accomplish, make their change an urgent priority.

Finally, a small tip to help solidify commitment: During this stage, your people will be watching you for signs of follow-up and consistency. Part of your strategy should be to respond to all rumors, questions, and concerns as quickly as possible. This is especially critical when the questions arise not from voices of resistance but reflect needful concerns that spring from the changes. Being fastidious in your follow-through will create a sense of consistency that will generate confidence in your people's capacity to change. Let your staff see you writing down things that need follow-up. Somehow, this is very reassuring.

LIVE IN THE LEAP

When one jumps over the edge,
one is bound to land somewhere.

—D. H. Lawrence

Eleven years ago when traveling with the circus, I had the opportunity to do something I'd always wanted to do. I went up on a flying trapeze. There I was, 60 feet in the air, standing on a tiny platform with a 260-pound man swinging opposite me. All (and I say that broadly) I had to do was swing out on the trapeze three times and let go of my bar. My momentum would carry me toward my catcher, who promised me he wouldn't fail.

After what felt like an eternity, I gathered the courage to propel myself off my little platform. Out I swung— once, twice, three times. When it was time to let go, only one thought crossed my mind: "I can't!" I continued to swing back and forth, clutching the bar, hanging on for what I believed was dear life. I just couldn't let go.

So there I was, swinging 60 feet above the ground, legs flapping, trying to keep my momentum and dignity intact. Eventually there came a time when the pain of embarrassment overcame my fear of death. I could hear my friends below, enjoying my humiliation, carrying on as if they were at a comedy show (which, looking back at it, I guess they were). Finally I decided, "To hell with it." I took a deep breath and let go of the bar, and, even though I'm Jewish, the only words that came from my lips were, "Oh Jesus, oh Jesus, oh Jesus . . ."

Of course, my momentum did exactly what I had been promised. I flew forward, was caught, and returned to my bar. Everything turned out just fine. But the memory of my fear, and the depth of strength it took to let go, is something I hold as especially powerful.

At a recent Johnson & Johnson executive roundtable discussion I attended, someone asked, "What does it take to be a truly fast-changing company?" Here are the answers we came up with: One, you need to align your systems, standards, and financial incentives across the company so that all are promoting the same outcomes; two, you need to have a truly integrated, state-of-the-art information system; and three, you need a willingness to make decisions before you have all the answers. In essence, you need to "live in the leap."

Most of us don't like to act until we know what our strategy for action is going to be. But given the rapidity of change in our world, that way of thinking just doesn't work any more. We suffer from FMS (fear of missing something). But to be truly effective, we must learn to deal comfortably with ambiguity. We can no longer wait until we have all the answers. We must act, and act decisively, even when certainty is lacking.

At some level, we are all like circus performers swinging on the trapeze. We are being asked, even implored, to let go of the bar. The problem is, not only don't we know whether someone is there to catch us, we may not know whether there is even another bar to grab. Still, we have no choice. We must let go or risk being left behind for good.

Letting go essentially requires two things. The first is the knowledge that the current situation is too painful to hold onto. You must realize or, as a leader, make your people realize that what they are currently grasping is no longer in their best self-interest. This requires honest and, at times, tough talk.

Second, there must be trust that, though the destination is unclear, the leap will be a safe one. Your people will not let go until they believe in you and the organization—until they believe that everything will be all right.

Living in the leap is an exercise in trust, not control. As E. L. Doctorow says about the practice of writing, "It's like driving in the fog. You may only see one headlight ahead at a time, but you can make the whole trip that way." Or as, Tennessee Williams wrote, "There is a time for departure, even when there's no certain place to go."

THE ONLY CONSTANT

**The one unchangeable certainty is that
nothing is unchangeable or certain.**

—John F. Kennedy

When Apollo Astronaut Neil Armstrong first walked on the moon, he not only uttered the famous words, "One small step for man, one giant leap for mankind," but also several other remarks, most of it the usual communication traffic among him, the other astronauts, and Mission Control in Houston.

But before he reentered the lunar lander, he made the enigmatic remark, "Good luck, Mr. Gorsky."

Many people at NASA thought it was a casual remark addressed, perhaps, to some rival Soviet cosmonaut; however, upon checking, they found that there was no Gorsky in either the Russian or American space programs.

Over the years, many people questioned Armstrong as to what the "Good luck, Mr. Gorsky" statement meant. He would never reply directly.

On July 5, 1995, in Tampa Bay, Florida, while Armstrong was answering questions following a speech, a reporter brought up the 26-year-old mystery. He finally explained. It seemed that Mr. Gorsky had died, and so Armstrong felt he could now tell the story.

"When I was a kid, I was playing baseball with my brother in the backyard. He hit a fly ball that landed in front of my neighbors' bedroom window. The neighbors were Mr. and Mrs. Gorsky. As I leaned down to pick up the ball, I heard Mrs. Gorsky shouting at Mr. Gorsky, "Oral sex? Oral sex you want? You'll get oral sex when the kid next door walks on the moon!"

As Mr. Gorsky's unimaginable good fortune reminds us, it's very clear that things will change. What we can't predict is *what* will change. Yet the simple awareness that change may be our only constant (besides death and taxes) helps us accept its inevitability, and thus helps us deal with its impact. Knowing that we are not alone in our struggles with change can help us move to a deeper level of acceptance.

Many times a simple statement from a leader, to the effect that "We're all going through an amazing amount of change," is enough to create a sense that everyone in the organization is facing the same struggles together. That alone can help.

Next time you're in the throes of yet another wave of seemingly unmanageable change, consider this quotation:

"We trained hard . . . but it seemed that every time we were beginning to form into teams we would be reorganized. I was later to learn in life that we tend to meet any new situation by reorganizing; and a wonderful method it can be for creating the illusion of progress while producing confusion, inefficiency, and demoralization."

Sound familiar? It's not an observation by Peter Drucker, Tom Peters, or even Scott Adams's Dilbert. It was written by Petronius the Arbiter, a Roman writer and politician who died in A.D. 66. Change has never been optional, and it never will be. The only option is how we respond, connect, and move forward into the future of our dreams.

PREPARE FOR THE WORST, EXPECT THE BEST

There is no security on this earth.
There is only opportunity.

—Douglas MacArthur

I was asked by the government of Northern Ireland to conduct a conflict-resolution process during the hunger strikes of the 1980s. The idea was to try to ease tensions in various Belfast neighborhoods and thereby let the peace process go forward without violence.

On my first night in Belfast, my Irish friends took me to a crowded pub in a mixed (Catholic and Protestant) area. My voice is a little high and nasal, and with my Philadelphia–South Jersey accent I stuck out like a sore thumb. Everything about me screamed "American."

At first, everything was fine; I was an object of mild, mostly friendly, curiosity, until, well into the evening, one drunken man decided to focus on me. He stumbled up to my table, interrupted our conversation, and demanded, "I see yer from the States. So tell me, what do ya think of the troubles here between the Protestants and the Catholics?"

Northern Ireland is a strange place. At the time, the country was very tense over profound political issues, yet no one, and I mean no one, ever discussed politics in public. The reason? You could be badly beaten, or worse, just for expressing an opinion. Knowing that people had been killed for discussing the current state of Ireland's political turmoil, I took the high road and kept my mouth shut. My Irish friends got very nervous and said to me, "Pay no attention to him, he's just drunk." But he wasn't just drunk, he was an angry drunk. The man spoke again, this time in a louder voice that clearly conveyed hostility.

"I said, Yank! What do you think of the troubles here in Belfast?"

By now, the entire pub was dead silent, all eyes upon me. Still I said nothing.

Now he began to roar. "I said, Yank! Tell me about the troubles between the Protestants and the Catholics— *now!*" And he slammed his fist on the table, making our glasses dance. His bloodshot eye was fixed on me in a ready-to-explode glare.

Slowly I rose from my seat, under the anxious scrutiny of my friends and the entire pub crowd. I stared the drunk down with my best John Wayne impression and slowly peeled off my jacket, revealing a T-shirt under-neath printed with the bold slogan, "DON'T SHOOT—I'M JEWISH!" (The T-shirt was a gift from friends before I left for Europe. It was a complete accident I happened to be wearing it that day.)

The pub full of people roared with laughter, as my challenger drew back in momentary surprise and confusion. When the noise died down, he gave me a broad wink, leaned toward me, and, in a hoarse stage whisper, demanded, "Aye! But are you a *Catholic* Jew or a *Protestant* Jew?!"

Again the pub roared. We were now among friends.

There is something about preparing for the worst that helps us manage the unexpected. Giving thought before-hand as to what could be the worst thing that could hap-pen can help you establish a game plan to deal with issues as they arise. Yet I'm continually amazed at how little real thought is given to considering the multitude of tough issues that will spring forth from any change. No matter how welcome the change may be, shifting sands always create shifting dynamics, which in turn will always bring headaches. Anticipating problems is crucially important.

On the other hand, as my friend Sandra Janoff says, it's important to avoid creating a negative prediction. We all know the studies that show predictive thinking tends to bring about what we predict. Act as if something bad will happen, and it usually does.

The trick, then, is to privately prepare for the all that can go wrong while publicly supporting your people with your belief in their best. It requires an open and honest awareness of each issue confronting you, not just a fantasy picture of hopes and fears. Is it easy? No. But it's essential.

One secret is to focus your language on the positives; talk about what you want, not on what you don't want. The subconscious rarely can tell the difference between the two. It sees only the image presented, regardless of framing, and moves toward it with deliberate speed. When you dwell on the downside, people will unconsciously begin to make it happen.

Here's a case in point. My friend Rod and I are very competitive in a friendly way. If we take a walk, we turn it into a race. We'll place bets on who can hit the stop sign with a snowball. At a lake, we'll have rock-skipping contests. Our competition is always good-natured, lively, and spirited—but intense.

Recently, we went to a driving range to see who could hit the golf ball the farthest. After several shots, I was in the lead, with Rod coming up for his last shot. I decided to use some subtle gamesmanship to ensure my victory. As Rod approached the ball, I muttered, barely audibly, "Whatever you do, don't hit it into the trees." I knew what I was doing. Of course, Rod shanked it straight into the woods.

Notice it didn't matter whether I said "Hit it into the trees" or "Don't hit it into the trees." The bottom line was, it was all about the trees. That's all Rod's subconscious heard—trees.

So when you're leading a change effort, always frame your language in terms of positive rather than negative outcomes. "I am looking forward to a smooth transition" is highly preferable to "Let's do our best to avoid a rocky start." It presents an image that ultimately will provoke the kind of supportive action you want. The difference is subtle, but can have profound effects.

By privately planning for the worst, but publicly calling on the best, you maximize your chances of covering all your bases.

OPENING UP MORE TIME

There will come a time when you
believe everything is finished.
That will be the beginning.

—Louis L'Amour

I recently enjoyed a lesson in time management from a most unexpected source. I was sitting at my dining room table one Thanksgiving, complaining about how I never had enough time in the day to do all the things I wanted to accomplish. My ten-year-old niece, Kimberly, batted her large brown eyes at me and said, "Well, you know what we learned in school, Uncle David?"

"What's that, sweetie?" I asked.

"We learned that Michelangelo, Leonardo da Vinci, Marie Curie, Thomas Edison, Mahatma Gandhi, and Martin Luther King all had exactly the same amount of time in a day that you do. Twenty-four hours!"

Nice kid.

But Kimberly had an important point. We often have more time than we think, if only we can respond to change in a different way. Our typical strategy, particularly if we tend to the more passive forms of resistance, is something like this: The change is announced. The date it is to be implemented is also given. Timelines are created and expectations established. In response, we deny, deny, deny, deny, right up until the eve of the deadline—then work like hell!

We can open up vast amounts of time if we take action on our changes earlier and more proactively. This is not to say that we have to remove all vestiges of denial. That would be unrealistic. And where would the fun be in that? But what if we could cut it in half? Or simply moved into action faster than usual? If we can consciously shift from our usual pattern of denial and inactivity toward active engagement, the results will be tangible. We could create a greater cushion of time, which in turn would enable us to work at a less frenzied pace.

A larger question remains, however, and that is why we procrastinate in the first place. Behind every procrastination lies one of two tendencies: perfectionism or weakheartedness. We hear within us a voice that is either afraid of failing or is so addicted to doing everything right that it doesn't want to risk looking foolish and so will choose not to act rather than take the risk of making a mistake.

When you find yourself procrastinating, look hard at your past achievements. Ask yourself questions like these:

"Where have I been successful in the past, and what skills and resources from those victories can be drawn upon for future work demands?"

"Where in the past have I built a successful track record that relates to the task at hand?"

"How can I apply my past successes to the tasks I face today?"

If you can use the answers to these questions to strengthen the internal framework through which you view your own skills and abilities, you will be much less reluctant to tackle projects or assignments that seem too challenging or difficult.

Most of us live in a kind of time warp anyway, unaware how far we have developed our own skills and abilities. The picture of who we think we are is very different from how we are seen by others. When we bolster our sense of self by examining our past successes, we build a foundation on which to move forward.

Manage the internal storm and the external project demands often get met.

WATCH THE WEATHER

Whoever you are. Some evening take a step out
of your house, which you know so well.
Enormous space is near . . .

—Rainer Maria Rilke

The great German poet and philosopher Goethe spent an hour every morning in his garden, dressed only in his nightshirt. He did this, he said, so he might better know the elements. The practice so sharpened his intuitive knowledge that he was able to predict the day's weather unfailingly. When he stopped this practice, he found that his forecasting abilities vanished.

There is something very powerful about being so close to our changing environment that we can unfailingly predict its behavior, so attuned that we can instinctively know what the future will be. Goethe knew. Through the simple act of standing outdoors in his nightshirt every morning, in rain, snow, sun, and wind, he was able to develop a sense of the day's future events that was extraordinarily accurate.

Often we become so myopically focused on our day-to-day tasks that we cannot sense around us the general ebb and flow of business life. What can you do to more closely attune your senses to your business environment?

It makes no difference whether we're considering business or weather forecasting—the principle is the same. You must take on the task of quietly watching your environment, as a respectful observer, to develop an intuitive sense of changes to come. When you stop doing that, you gradually begin to lose your ability to predict changes.

Spend half an hour every day in your place of business, simply watching. Look around you and sense the changes in internal company weather that are everywhere. Like nature, an organization has many moods. Try to understand what they are, not by "figuring" but just by observing. Take the role of the "fair witness," an observer who sees without judgment. Try not to evaluate what is going on. You will have the rest of your day for that. Just watch, as a country person watches the weather. What storm fronts or cloud heads do you see approaching? What is the temperature? Where is it hot? Cold? Sticky? Blustery?

Just remember, this is a practice in being neutral. A wise Yogi once said, "Observation without evaluation is the highest form of spiritual practice." The spirit you want to bring to this exercise is one of curiosity. For every observation that triggers a strong emotional response, simply say to yourself, "Isn't that interesting." Don't judge. Neutral observation is the key to prediction.

This exercise not only will help you learn to anticipate the changing weather of your organization, it will help you still your own internal storms whenever they arise. And they will.

SEEK EXCELLENCE,
NOT PERFECTION

You will do many foolish things in your life.
So do them with enthusiasm.

—Colette

There is a world of difference between perfection and excellence. Perfection doesn't tolerate mistakes; excellence incorporates mistakes. During times of change and transition, it is impossible not to make mistakes. That is the nature of change. It is always evolutionary and, by definition, evolution modifies and builds upon errors from the past.

Consider the words of these leaders and innovators: Lincoln: "We learn more from what has not been done right, than what has been done right." Edison: "The secret is not the 71 times you fail, but to persevere to the 72nd time, in which you succeed." Gandhi: "Only a fool expects perfection. A wise man seeks learning."

The key question is this: How can you build an excellence mentality in your organization rather than a perfection mentality? A perfection mentality will serve only to freeze thinking. It introduces an element of fear, which limits risk-taking and acts of bravery. It paralyzes instead of liberates, constricts instead of expands. The cruel paradox is that, if we have a perfection-driven mind-set when we most need creative, adventurous thinking, we will, out of fear, play it safe instead.

Imagine that you are an airline pilot. Did you know that if you fly from, let's say, New York to Chicago, most of the time you are off-course? *Off-course* is defined in aviation as not exactly on your flight plan coordinates. Of course, you are usually within the flight corridor, a huge swath of sky that falls within acceptable standards. When told he's off-course by the navigator or tower, the pilot doesn't get upset, self-berating, or angry. Instead, he just responds, analyzes where he needs corrective action, and behaves appropriately. The information becomes data that allows for course correction—without emotion or judgment.

So the question remains: How do we achieve this mind-set?

Here's one simple recommendation: Every two weeks as you are going through a major change initiative, pull your people together and ask two simple questions: "What mistakes have you made these past two weeks?" and "What have you learned from them?" This second question is critical, for it builds in what management guru Peter Senge refers to as a "Learning Culture."

If your people are not coming to you with any mistakes, you will know one of two things. Either they are not making any—which means they are not growing, developing, or changing—or they are getting really good at covering them up. Both should be unacceptable.

Of course, make sure that every meeting includes your "learnings," and that you carefully model appreciation for the insights and struggles that your folks are going through. It won't take too many critical comments following the revelation of a mistake for people to shut back down into a perfection mode.

WORK YOUR PROBLEMS SYSTEMICALLY

We look at art from 360 degrees. The only problem is we forgot to do that with our lives.

—Andy Warhol

Believe it or not, a surprisingly large number of people who have been blind from birth, upon gaining their sight through an operation, ask to have it taken away again. Why? One theory is that they can't handle seeing the whole picture at once. A dog isn't a dog, but a nose, ears, tail, and legs. Those who have been blind struggle with the concept of a "whole dog," with seeing the system of interconnections that make the whole.

We're equally shortsighted when it comes to understanding the whole systems that make up our organizations and the problems and challenges they face. The old view, to which most of us cling, is that we can list our problems and solve them one by one, like checking off items on a shopping list. Unfortunately, when you follow the shopping-list approach, solving one problem usually creates another problem. Your solution just becomes the next problem. Or, as is often the case, *my* solution becomes *your* next problem.

The fact is that all problems and their eventual resolution are interrelated. Therefore, a strategy that looks at the interrelationships of problems and their solutions is essential. We have all heard the saying, "How do you eat an elephant? One bite at a time." Organizational change is like that—except the elephant changes after every bite.

To draw a different analogy, the process of change is less like a march and more like dancing a polka. On a march, you set your target and you go forward toward it; the process is linear, focused, and systematic. (It's also usually pretty boring.) By contrast, if you're doing the polka (say, at one of those wonderful Polish weddings), the steps are more like, "One, two, side step, back, one two, side step, back." Furthermore, as you avoid the other dancers, you are constantly wheeling and checking out your environment, moving forward and backward, making progress around the room, but in a nonlinear fashion.

If you expect linear progress during change, you will be sorely disappointed. Expect something more like a polka—energetic, fun, and unpredictable.

General Von Molte, the great Polish strategist, once said, "No battle plan survives the first contact." (Maybe he'd danced his share of polkas.) The keys are *flexible awareness* and a willingness to assume that you are a piece of a web that impacts a greater whole. Change just your piece of the dance and you will inevitably get into trouble by stepping on someone else's toes or disrupting the entire dance floor.

Every time you change something in any organization, large or small, you have to take a step back, look at the entire situation, and ask, "Who else will be affected by this action? How do I get them involved early on? How do I keep the various stakeholders linked to each other?" Then act on the results of this analysis.

It all requires a willingness to seek full understanding before you implement solutions. Push to understand the complexity of everything that is involved and avoid the tendency to rush into action without fully understanding the impact of change.

INPUT DOES NOT EQUAL OWNERSHIP

Not everything that counts can be counted.
Not everything that can be counted counts.

—Albert Einstein

Sometimes it seems we Americans are in love with the input process. Consulting firms have gotten very wealthy using input as a key strategy for change. We've developed a host of methods, scientific and otherwise, for gathering people's opinions and ideas: focus groups, assessments, audits, attitude surveys, and the list goes on and on. (This isn't true only in business, of course. It's even more prevalent in public policy. Many politicians won't dare to pick a place to eat lunch without having the results of public opinion polls backing their choice of restaurant.)

The intention—to involve the opinions of others—is good, but the process is flawed and often ineffective. The problem with the process of assessment is that it does not connect the providers of input to their own data. And without connection, there is no ownership. In fact, the opposite is often true.

This truth—that input does not equal ownership—stunned me when I first realized it. In fact, it went against all my professional training. But over time, I began to learn that the process of gathering input often helps to *block* effective change!

When individuals merely provide input, they also give away their responsibility to fix or do anything about the situation. Somehow, the problem you are asking about stays *your* problem. The thinking seems to go something like this: "You've asked for my opinion, and I've given it. Now good luck with your problem. And, by the way, don't think this means I'll support your change effort."

Apparently being asked to provide input is a passive process, so the commitment to change will also be passive.

That's why so many well-intentioned attempts to involve people through focus groups or surveys are a failure.

The key to meaningful change is not input. The key is *engagement*. By creating active dialogues where everybody hears everything and where all the members of the group are encouraged to wrestle with the full dimensions of the problem, you start to build that sense of engagement.

I am not opposed to data collection as a means of giving leadership information upon which to act. I use the process quite a bit in my own practice. But, and this is a big but, it can never be used as the sole strategy to engage a disenfranchised workforce.

Engagement is built when individuals work on real problems that involve their interests and the common good of the organization. Shared work with shared results implies shared ownership—something that will never be achieved by the passive approach of data collection.

We live in complicated times. If our problems were simple, we would have solved them by now. The solutions will arise only from engaged ownership at multiple levels. And this occurs only when key employees and organizational leaders understand that only by working together in new and different ways can they hope to solve the complex problems they face. It demands real communication, without intermediaries like surveys and consultant-run focus groups to interpret and simplify.

SEEK COMMON GROUND

Out beyond the world of ideas of right doing
and wrong doing, there is a field.
I will meet you there.

—Jellaludin Rumi

Seeking common ground is the process of looking for similarities in dialogue rather than differences. Imagine two partially interlocking circles. Where they overlap is the common ground. In any dialogue on change, common ground always exists despite the potential conflicts. Your job during change efforts is to find that common ground and maximize its power.

When we focus on differences, we are usually drawn into conversations regarding the past. "He said/she said" arguments arise, focused on what has happened, not on what could be. Studies show that when people become past-focused, they generally get depressed. Similarly, focusing on differences depletes our energy and leaves us mired in patterns of conflict and anxiety. When we shift our focus to common ground instead, we typically find our vision shifting to the future. Our conversations focus on what could be, creating energy and hope.

During the late 1980s, monumental changes occurred in South Africa, centering on the dismantling of the evil system of apartheid and the granting of political power to the country's black majority. These remarkable accomplishments, achieved through mainly peaceful means, were possible only because the leaders on all sides of the conflict focused on the future. Both Nelson Mandela and P. W. Botha knew that to focus on past conflicts, the pain they'd caused, and the fear in which the white minority had been living, would be unfruitful. Instead, they spent most of their time looking to the future of South Africa, not its past. Only when they focused on what they wanted for the country they both loved were they able to cross the barriers that had locked their people in conflict for decades. Common-ground thinking produced historic change.

This is not to say that we deny conflicts when they occur. In fact, whenever you bring passionate and creative people together with strong beliefs, you will usually have conflict. But you can acknowledge differences without always working them. *Working a conflict* means spending a lot of time and effort on issues you believe have little potential for resolution. Days, weeks, even months can be wasted working issues that will never be settled. It's like scratching an itch—tempting and superficially satisfying, yet the more you scratch, the redder and more painful the irritated spot becomes.

You'll find that very few people have the energy to fix anything when they are busy fighting over their differences. Only where common ground exists are people ready, willing, and able to take action and move forward.

Why waste time arguing over our areas of disagreement? Let's instead focus on areas where we agree, and watch the shifts that occur in both of our thinking when we build on common ground.

GET THE WHOLE SYSTEM IN THE ROOM

It's all very well in practice,
but it will never work in theory.

—French management principle

When creating a dialogue about change, get the whole system into the room.

Once established as a protocol, this concept can forever shift the way you do business.

The premise is a simple but profound one. In the past, a problem in shipping was usually dealt with in the shipping department. If you had a change to make in how you worked with a customer, you worked just with the customer. But with the advent of "whole systems thinking," based on the work of people like Eric Trist, Fred Emory, and Marvin Weisbord, we started to take a hard look at the ineffective results that were coming from this approach. Could we do things differently—and better?

Fact is, without the benefit of the whole picture, the solutions we created were usually disappointing. Slowly, we learned that effective systems of change involve a larger context than the one we're used to seeing. How can you look at shipping without looking at sales, manufacturing, accounting, and so on? How can you solve a customer's problem without considering how the change will affect your suppliers, your marketing people, and many others? Thanks to this new insight, the goal became to broaden out organizational perceptions, seeing each problem within its larger context.

Here's an example. When tackling a major change project with a healthcare organization, we decided to convene a three-day conference looking at the future of the organization's role in the industry. But rather than inviting just a few top executives, we chose to bring together everyone who'd be affected by the vision and the decisions to be crafted—"the whole system," in short. We had stakeholder groups representing physicians, administration, nurses, hospital workers, patients, the community, insurance companies, vendors, and the government, all talking together, working together to shape the organization's future.

By doing this as one event, as opposed to the typical strategy of creating a task force that goes out into the system to gather data, we avoided some common problems.

First, a task force usually misses the benefit of the "whole" perspective. Individual viewpoints never get the opportunity to expand due to the input of others, and same-group myopia is only reinforced. This is the problem with focus groups. They are fine for gathering data about what *is,* but often ineffective for creating a glimpse of what *could be.* In a focus group, for example, line workers will discuss only the line worker viewpoint and will rarely be able to move beyond their current thinking. Real breakthroughs can happen only when interested parties are brought to the table with views different than their own.

Remember, if the solution were easy, you would have thought of it by now. As Einstein said, "The problems we face cannot be solved at the level of thinking we were at when we created them." The goal must be to create a process that expands viewpoints and perspectives, allowing new solutions, rather than reinforcing constrictive thinking.

Getting the right people into the room takes work, but the payoff can be felt in unexpected ways. Bringing in outside stakeholders adds value into the process. Besides broadening the views of your internal people, you also start to shift the civility level of all involved. Having "guests" in the room can create powerful behavioral changes in typical meeting behavior. Sessions that usually end up with one internal group aggressively confronting another are significantly more civil when the whole system is present. Whether it feels like "best behavior" or not is of little consequence. The key is that a pattern is broken, new ways of talking are encouraged and practiced, and a different process is created. This establishes an organizational memory over time that can shift your internal communication patterns.

The second issue that arises if you don't have the whole system present is that a lot of time is spent talking about who's not there. This can become a major source of unproductive energy spent asking questions such as, "Well, it's not a bad idea, but what would the people in shipping think?" A corollary to this is that plans are sometimes made for those not present, who then get angry because they weren't involved and find ways of resisting whatever plans were made without their participation. Understandably, those who worked hard on the process then get frustrated with the lack of commitment and paint the uninvited as naysayers or obstructionists. The circle of anger gets reestablished. Getting all involved groups around the same table prevents this.

Finally, there often will be problems implementing significant changes when the few plan for the many. Whenever possible, plan *with* others, not *for* others. When small task forces go forth, collect data, and make recommendations, they are inevitably put in the position of having to "sell" the idea to the rest of the organization. This is why so many expensive consulting plans end up in binders on the shelves of the CEO's office. There has been precious little cultural change to allow the process to move forward throughout the real world of the company.

Never forget this truth: *A plan is not doing. Doing is doing.* That's why small groups trying to influence large, uninvolved stakeholders with little or no investment rarely accomplish much.

When you involve everyone, you have the system fixing the system. It's harder work at first, but the payoff comes at implementation. So, as you move forward with your change process, always ask the question, "Do we have the right people in the room?" Push the level of involvement so it reflects the whole system at any one time.

ACKNOWLEDGE DIFFERENCES, THEN ACT

Memories fade. They were designed that way.

—Unknown

My friend and colleague Nancy Aronson once made a profound and elegant statement during a particularly tense meeting. With the group stuck in an argument over a particularly tough issue, she quietly commented, "You don't need to agree on everything before you can start taking action." Eyes widened, wheels began to turn, and the dynamics of the moment shifted to bold action from entrenched defensiveness.

While Nancy's Law may seem basic, the truth of the matter is that many times we shut down dialogue over disagreements rather than hang in with each other and make progress where we can. When we have the persistence to build on what is working, the momentum will eventually affect those areas that are not working.

Imagine holding an orange in your right hand and an apple in your left. The fruit represent two divergent points of views: the apple represents the way I see the world, while the orange represents how you see the world. Now imagine placing both pieces of fruit on the floor next to you, one on your left and one on your right. You can't see both; in fact, until something changes, you may never be able to bring both views together. But if you take a single step forward, away from the fruit, and then look back, your perspective changes. You have created forward momentum away from your entrenched, hard-fought position, and now both views can be embraced in a single broader perspective.

This is what happens when people temporarily put aside their differences to work with their areas of agreement. Progress happens, and as a result, perspectives begin to change. Formerly bitter adversaries now enjoy the benefit of some distance from the most contentious issues as well as the history of success that comes from acting together.

Is this an idealistic fantasy? Not at all. Think for a moment of some of the powerful adversaries who have turned into partners: the United States and Japan; Apple and IBM; managers and employees of Saturn. Not only have these former opponents found common ground, but they've been able to leverage their learnings into new and exciting forms of progress.

One of the great truths of life is that feelings and emotion tend to shift, even when we do nothing to shift them. Thus, there is great power in simply hanging on, and moving where we can jointly move. In the end, the building of trust through common ground can allow us to work through even the most contentious differences.

Consider the most difficult and confrontational situations you currently face. Who are they with? Where does common ground exist where you can jointly take action? What successes can the two of you create that may lead to a stronger partnership at a later time?

It is not just politics that makes strange bedfellows. When we act for our common benefit, the whole world can start to change.

TAPPING YOUR INTERNAL WISDOM

Even the largest corporation can be too small for the hopes and desires of one human soul.

—David Whyte

As someone who makes a living as an organizational consultant, I probably shouldn't be saying this, but we've become a society that is consultant- and expert-dependent. When confronted with a serious problem, our first instinct all too often is to look for some outside guru who can guide us through it. As a result, we forget to seek out the internal wisdom that may already exist in the people with whom we live and work every day.

Not only is this consultant-dependency inefficient, but it also disregards the uniqueness of every challenge we and our organizations face, assuming instead that what we need is some expert with a prepackaged solution. We should be moving away from dependency on outside experts and recognize that the unique nature of every system demands specific responses that only internal wisdom can truly know.

I often recall the words of my first mother-in-law, who when someone called my house and asked for Dr. Baum, responded, "Well, yes, he's in. But I should warn you, he's not the kind of doctor who can do anybody any good!" While I didn't appreciate the specifics of the comment, I had to agree with the sentiment. Don't rely on experts (even those with Ph.D.s). The changing nature of most industries requires unique solutions, not prefab ones.

In more than 20 years of research on social and technical change in organizations, only two critical findings have consistently emerged. One is that 85 percent of the expertise needed to create most organizational solutions is already present in the organization. And the second is that, when an employee-conceived plan fails, it is usually because senior leadership didn't trust the plan and meddled with it.

The two findings are connected, of course. It takes a huge leap of faith for leadership to believe that the knowledge exists, if they are only willing to believe it. One key is simply to ask. During the making of the classic movie *The Wizard of Oz*, a particular song found its way to the cutting-room floor. The producers and director had decided to delete it from the movie, considering it, frankly, no better than second rate. Fortunately, something inside MGM producer David O. Selznick led him to question the decision. Late one night in his office, he played the clip for the cleaning woman and asked her what she thought. She loved it, and Selznick decided to trust her instincts. The next day, Judy Garland's rendition of "Over the Rainbow" was restored to the movie, despite the opinions of the "leaders" and "experts" around the studio.

Ask yourself: What untapped wisdom exists in your organization? Who have you not asked that may have the answers to some of your most troubling issues? Go to the sources you never visit—not the same voices, but new and different ones. As the saying goes, "If you always do what you've always done, you'll always get what you've always got."

WALK YOUR TALK

We convince by our presence.

—Walt Whitman

A wonderful story is told about Horst Shultze, the president of Ritz-Carlton Hotels. A number of years ago, Shultze wanted to get his organization aligned to the mission and vision he'd created for the Ritz. He initiated a year-long training program concerning customer service and the Ritz-Carlton mission, which every employee at the 13 Ritz-Carlton hotels went through. It was a massive effort costing hundreds of thousands of dollars.

When the program was completed, Shultze pulled the general managers of all 13 hotels into a conference room and made the following request: "We have just spent a lot of time and money to train our employees on the mission statement of the Ritz. Would you please take out a piece of paper and write it for me?"

Out of 13 general managers at that meeting, 7 could repeat the mission statement, but 6 could not. If you were Horst Shultze, what would you have done? Whenever I've asked this question to large groups of managers, the overwhelming response has always been, "Fire them!" Of course! It's a natural response. But Schultze had a different reaction. He offered to resign. Schultze was personally humiliated for his own failure to make it clear what he wanted, and he assumed full responsibility for the problem and was willing to suffer the consequences for it. You can imagine the uproar.

Of course, Schultze stayed on. The general managers got the message in a very powerful way. And a few years later, the Ritz-Carlton Hotels won the Malcolm Baldrige Award, the national prize for business excellence.

To this day, managers at the Ritz-Carlton chain point to that moment in time as the seminal one that changed the company's sense of ownership of the mission. It was at that meeting that a message was clearly sent: Our leaders walk their talk.

Today, if you walk into any Ritz-Carlton Hotel in the world and ask any employee what their company's mission statement is, you will very likely get the answer. It is deeply ingrained in the culture. Few organizations in this world can make the same claim. Can you recite your own organization's mission statement? At the Ritz, they can because they all know that, when it comes to the Ritz mission, Horst Schultze says what he means and does what he says.

Harvard researchers John Kotter and Jim Heskett have shown that the single most important factor distinguishing successful corporate change efforts from those that fail is effective and competent leadership. Without clear, focused leadership that sets an example of personal commitment, most change efforts will fall far short of expectations. Kotter and Heskett also found that, when change efforts fail, it is because leadership undercommunicates their vision for the future—not slightly, but, on average, by a factor of ten!

If your change effort is to be successful, leadership must be totally visible and totally involved. Your employees have a very sensitive built-in B.S. meter. They watch more than they listen. Your credibility depends on your ability to convince your employees that you will fully commit to modeling not only *what* will change but *how* it will change. That is the bottom line. It requires courage, conviction, and an honest appraisal of your strengths and limitations.

In one famous study, business executives were asked, "What do you value most in your lives?" Most responded, "My children." The researchers then shadowed these same executives to determine how much time each one spent one-on-one, face-to-face with their son or daughter. The average was 8 to 12 minutes per week! This with their kids who they said they valued the most! (For comparison, consider that the average American spends four to six hours per day watching television—and 45 minutes to an hour per day in the bathroom!)

We are not what we say. We are what we do. I know it. You know it. And most important, your employees know it. If you ask of your people what you yourself are not ready, willing, and able to commit to right now, your change effort is dead in the water, even before you start.

MOVEMENT HAPPENS WHEN WE GIVE THINGS UP

The mastery can be gained by letting things go their own way. It can't be gained by interfering or controlling.

—Lao-tzu

Sometimes with senior teams I play a simulation, adapted from Alex Bavelas, called "Broken Squares." Each participant in a group of five is given between two and three cut pieces of cardboard and told the following:

"You have two tasks. Your individual task is to form a perfect square in front of you on the table. Your group task is to make sure that each individual meets his or her individual task. You will have succeeded when everyone has a perfect square in front of them that are all the same size and at the same time."

Of course, the only way this can be done is to mix and match the different cardboard pieces. The kicker is this: There are about eight different ways individual squares can be made, but only one way all the squares can be made at the same time.

Added to the task are the following two rules: no team member may speak or gesture during the exercise, and you may only give pieces away and may not take pieces. This last part is very challenging. It's amazing to watch what happens when one person gets a square completed but forgets the group task. The person guards his or her square with an "I've got mine" look and watches as others try and struggle to complete theirs. The problem is they usually have a square made with pieces needed by other team members to finish their squares. If the wrong combination occurs in the first square, the group task will never get completed until he or she breaks up their square and passes the pieces out for a new combination.

Initially the impact is hilarious. Because no talking or pointing is allowed, team members who see the dilemma have this imploring look in their eyes. They often stare at the unwavering team member with his or her completed square. The amazing paradox is this. The team members with the completed squares are often least likely to see the dilemma. They guard their successes and close down any options for alternative thinking. It's amazing to see well compensated executives, who are paid to see the big picture, unconsciously cover their cardboard pieces with their arms. Breakthrough only occurs when they understand the pattern and break apart their square to pass to other team members.

Sometimes they get it quickly and sometimes they can struggle on this simple problem for 30 to 45 minutes, but the essential learning is this: Movement only occurs when I give something up; movement never occurs when I refuse to give away or take. This simple insight has myriad profound implications.

Every change brings with it conflict. That is inevitable. How then do you create movement when intractable positions refuse to budge? Often the root can be traced to leaders who hold firm to their viewpoints and don't offer to give something up. Yet the key to any resolution is often the willingness of one party to step forward and "give away" what they have (money, power, authority) for the common good. It is the essential breakthrough point in political tension, union negotiation, or team development. If positions are guarded, movement rarely occurs.

As a leader, deeply question where and when you can "give away." It can be as broad as authority on a project or first offering apology and owning what you did wrong *without expectation* the other party will do the same. When we model generosity, we create the capacity for people to rise to another level of behavior. That, after all, is what will create the fastest change.

FIND THE MEANING IN IT ALL

Those who are drawn to the music are thought insane by those who can't hear it.

—Unknown

The president of a children's hospital I know has an enviable option every time he is fed up with the daily crap of his job. He visits the cancer unit. There among the kids with life-threatening illness he replenishes his spirit and energy. He told me once, "Every time I feel sorry for myself I just spend time with those kids. Some people would find it emotionally hard to walk among all these children with cancer—but not me. It puts me back in touch with what I do and why. When dealing with tough board members or physicians I just remember what we're *really* in business for. I get fired up again and go back and fight the good fight."

When all else fails, finding a sense of meaning in it all is not just important, but is critical to survival. During times of great change and frustration, return in your mind to what gives meaning to your work. Ask yourself: What is it in my job that gives me pride and value? Where does the mission of my job move me? Every profession has its calling. It is the nature of the human spirit to find such meaning no matter how mundane the work or how difficult the situation.

One famous study looked at the mundane existence of factory workers who were responsible for wrapping light bulbs in tissue paper. What the researchers found was that each worker developed a slightly different wrapping pattern, experimented with it and frequently changed it, as if to bring a sense of themselves and their unique personality into their work. Undaunted, the creative will find a way to express itself.

I once sat next to the then-governor of New Hampshire, Steve Merrill, on a plane. I asked him how he balanced the pressures of his job. "When things get a bit much, I tell my secretary I'm going to play golf. And then I go home and spend time with my kids."

"Why do you do that?" I asked.

"Because sadly, in today's world, golf is an acceptable excuse for taking time off and spending time with your kids isn't. So rather than deal with other people's judgments, I say I'm heading to the golf course and instead drive straight home."

During a difficult time of change, challenge yourself to examine where you are replenished emotionally by what you do. It may be the job itself, the people you serve or interact with, the family you help support, or some other blessing no one else would even notice. No matter what it may be, it's at the heart of what keeps us going. Use it to fuel your spirit, as others have.

WHAT YOU CHANGE, HOW YOU CHANGE

Presentation is everything.

—Inuit saying

I once saw a quotation scrawled on an outhouse wall (don't ask) that said, "In how you do anything, is how you do everything."

How you go about creating change will be reflected in the process you use. I am constantly amazed to see organizations adopting a change process that is antithetical to the results they want. It is one of the great paradoxes of business that defies any rational thought. For instance, I've worked with organizations that want to build a culture that pushes ownership down to the broadest levels by creating a strong sense of point-of-service accountability. Leadership's intention was to embolden those throughout the organization to make important decisions and take ownership accordingly. It's a fine goal. But these organizations then try to go about creating this new culture by mandating it!

It makes no sense, of course. If you want an empowered workforce, the process of change you use to make the journey must be an empowering one. The rule is this: Whatever you do must match the desired results you are trying to create. In most traditional business models, the process simply does not.

Often we get the right task, or the right task and the right people. But rarely do we get an alignment of the three legs of the stool—task, people, and the right process.

So consider carefully not just what you want to change but how you want to change. You cannot, for instance, get a team-based culture by rewarding performance on an exclusively individual basis. If you want people to think outside their personal interest you must reward accordingly. Or you cannot create a culture of speed by punishing for mistakes. If you want speed, than you must allow your people to explore and learn from error. Or you cannot create a strategic plan that fosters interdependency by writing it at a mountain top retreat with five people and a consultant. I could go on forever. Think long and hard about the messages you are sending through the ways you pursue change. Ask yourself how the process will help to create the outcomes you are trying to deliver. Right people and right task is the easy part. But does your process match the results you want to create?

General Norman Schwartzkopf, the acclaimed leader of Operation Desert Storm, once said, "The plan is unimportant. Planning is everything." How we get to where we want to go is as important as the destination. In most change efforts, the target is always moving. But what we learn from the how will ultimately serve us long after the what has been accomplished.

PRACTICE BRAVERY

There is a time for departure,
even when there's no certain place to go.

—Tennessee Williams

As it does in our personal lives, change in our organizations requires a level of bravery that can be a test of our mettle. Finding the necessary resolve is not easy. As my wise friend Angeles Arrien once told me, "Change is not for sissies." Getting comfortable with ambiguity and uncertainty of change is a prerequisite for leading others through the maze. You must be able to look into the eyes of those you are leading and be able to say, "Everything will be all right." If you can't, why would they follow? But saying those words—and meaning them—takes courage.

Of course, the way most of us live is such that we rarely feel comfortable with change. We're creatures of habit. We dress the same, travel the same way to work, talk to our kids the same way: "How was school today?" "Fine." Our lives become exercises in ritual. We actually discourage a sense of comfort with change, and instead prefer predictability and sameness.

How can you increase your comfort level with change? The old joke still holds true: "Can you tell me how to get to Carnegie Hall?" "Practice, practice, practice!"

So practice bravery and change. The Basque people of northern Spain celebrate their birthdays once a month, instead of once a year, by doing something they've never done before. This way, when a whole year passes, they'll know they've faced the unknown 12 times. Such a life is a very helpful preparation for change.

Here's a favorite story of mine, one that exemplifies the benefit of bravery in a changing environment. It's presented the way it was told at an "all hands" company meeting by a midlevel manager in manufacturing.

We were being asked to change the ways we had been working. Change was happening quickly, but we were all quite resistant to many of the ideas that were being passed down. A number of seminars on change were presented, but frankly, they were a bit flat. We didn't believe we could do it.

One day, all 60 of the managers were brought together without warning and introduced to a new consultant—David Baum. We expected some kind of talk on management or communications, but instead David promised he could teach all of us to *juggle*—and furthermore, that he could do it within one hour! You should have seen the looks of disbelief and shock on our faces when we realized he was dead serious. However, he seemed unaffected by our pessimism. He pulled out a huge bag of colorful scarves, which he proceeded to pass around, instructing each of us to take three.

Working step by step, he had every single manager in that room juggling within 45 minutes—15 minutes ahead of schedule! We were roaring with laughter. We took pictures, teased each other—it was great. We still talk about it two years later. And guess what? We rarely are caught saying, "I can't do that" any more. And we keep those scarves on our desks as a reminder of the Great Juggling Symposium and the lesson it taught us.

Practice facing the unknown in a consistent way. Take time to try something new as often as possible; it doesn't matter what it is, as long as it's something you've never done before. Do you avoid making speeches? Place yourself in front of a group and talk about something that interests you. Never been on Rollerblades? Get a set and learn to skate. Can't carry a tune? Take singing lessons. You don't need to go to India to get a strong and important benefit from expanding your personal horizons.

To maximize the benefits, stay conscious of your emotions and reactions as you face your personal challenges. Start a log of lessons learned and relearned. You will be amazed at their relevance to the organizational changes you face. By getting comfortable with small changes, you prepare yourself to lead others through big changes.

BEWARE OF CROSS-PURPOSES

Leadership has a harder job than to choose sides. It must bring sides together.

—Jesse Jackson

I served a recent consulting engagement with a Fortune 50 company that was converting its information system to SAP, a proprietary business processing and operational database software program—a $50 million investment. The project was being managed through a

lead control center and four "customer" groups that rep-
resented the four major divisions of the company. I'd
been hired to help with the transition process in the largest of these divisions.

It became painfully obvious during the process of
working with the control center that their goals and purposes were very different from ours. Their motto was,
"On time, under budget." Not a bad theme, until you
started to peel back its implications.

"On time, under budget" is all about reaching a finish
line at a certain date. And appropriately enough, the
whole system at the control center was set up to reward a
fast and furious finish. Every decision they made, every
action they took, reflected this orientation. Most of the
team from the control center was scheduled to disband
the day after "cut-over" to the new system. Their outside
consultants (a team from one of the Big Five accounting
firms) were also scheduled to leave the same day, with the
added incentive of a huge bonus if they hit their numbers
and met the target date. "Let's put this thing to bed!"
became the watchword for the group.

Yet the divisions were operating with a different set of
goals. Their primary purpose was to have a *successful*
implementation, because they knew they were going to
be left with whatever mess was created by a rush-to-the-
finish approach. For them, the real work would start the
day after cut-over, when all hell would break loose—when
any flaws, errors, and confusions in the system would

become apparent, affecting operations throughout the division.

Thus, successful implementation was the theme reflected in everything they did, from the pacing of decisions ("Let's get it right") to the way information was requested ("Why don't they want our input?").

It didn't take long for conflicts to arise. The control center folks were seen by the divisional staffers as being distant and unwilling to support the needs of the field. The divisions were seen by the control center people as slow, timid, and stubborn. Under the stress of disagreement and growing hostility, good people began to make bad decisions. It was a mess.

All of this could have been avoided had some time been spent up front with all the teams in one room examining the purposes of the project. However, the control center team believed that decision making needed to be centralized, and that any open discussion of goals and expectations would, at best, be a deterrent to achieving the all-important deadline.

The consultants' Big Five firm, noted for its centralized approach, shared this view. Steeped in arrogance and unchecked power, the control center team almost never visited the customer sites; when they did, they shut themselves off in a meeting room and spoke with only one or two people. One result was a lack of simple awareness at the most basic level. For instance, critical members of the implementation team had never even met the head of the project. Despite a yearlong change effort that cried out for strong coordination and communication, they had no idea what the divisional change leader even looked like! The message this sent was powerful—and sad.

The bottom line? "On time, under budget" carried the day. And the day after cut-over, the problems created were substantial and profound. The control center was totally unprepared for the chaos that resulted, and most of the system's end-users in the company were left angry and mistrustful. Not only that, but the support systems that should have been in place didn't exist. The company ground to a halt for weeks, leaving scars that are still healing.

And the Big Five consultants? The day after cut-over, they were off to their next assignment.

When you're moving forward with any organizational change, large or small, be sure everyone is on the same page regarding purposes and goals. Don't take what people say at face value; really take time to examine the spoken and unspoken agendas of all your key players. Make implicit goals explicit, and create ongoing opportunities for dialogue among all those involved.

Had anyone from the control center really looked at the implications of "On time, under budget" and the messages it sent to their internal customers, the headlong rush to confusion could have been averted.

Ask the questions. It may be the single smartest move you ever make.

TWO MAGICAL WORDS

You can go a long way before finding
out you've been wrong.

—Unknown

A number of years ago, I was called into a rehabilitation hospital in crisis. Nineteen out of 25 department heads of the hospital had marched into the chairman of the board's office to complain about the hospital president. They declared, "Either he goes or we go." The chairman, in his infinite wisdom, thought, "We have a problem," and then he called me.

The history sets the context. Twenty years earlier, the hospital had been a nursing home with some 50 beds. Back then they had hired a hot young administrator with poor social skills but a huge vision and appetite for success. Howard (not his real name) drove change in the organization, growing the little nursing home into a preeminent 300-bed rehab facility known for a very specialized form of care. It had a national reputation and a unique and growing market niche. By all outside accounts, it (and he) was a huge success.

The problem was that Howard grew the organization on the backs of his staff. He was unrelenting in his drive, pushing his staff to the brink of exhaustion and burnout time and time again. He cared nothing for feelings or the impact of his decisions on human lives; his only interest was the growth and potential of the organization. The board was delighted; they saw growth and a healthy bottom line. But you can only go so far with such a strategy before the consequences start to accumulate. Now the bubble was about to burst.

Obviously, no matter how terrific you may think your president is, losing 75 percent of your management staff is an unacceptable cost. I was called in to see if I could help fix the problem.

After two days of one-on-one interviews with the staff, it was painfully obvious to me that the president was in deep trouble. I had strangers crying in front of me, shaking with rage and emotionally stricken over his behavior. These were dedicated and caring people who loved their work, their profession, and each other. They had hung in for as long as they could, and had now collectively reached a wall.

I'll never forget the meeting I had with Howard and the board chair in the president's office. "You have a serious problem," I said, "but you may be able to create hope from this difficult situation if you are willing to go in front of your entire staff and say two simple words: 'I'm sorry.' Can you do that?"

"Of course," Howard responded. "That's easy."

"Are you sure?" I again asked. "You must mean it and convey that to your staff. Otherwise, you will not be able to turn this situation around. As it is, you have, at best a 50/50 shot."

"No problem," he shot back. "I am truly sorry for what I did, and I will say so."

Somehow, I was less than convinced, and told him so. He reassured me that he was sorry and he would say so—and that was all he would say. So we went ahead. This was the hand we'd been dealt, and we'd all see how it played out.

Two hours later, we were in a large conference room with all the managers, the chairman, the president, and myself. First the chairman spoke, but the managers were only faintly interested in what he had to say. Then I spoke about what I had found. Interest went up slightly, but only because they wanted to know if I was truthfully going to repeat in the large group what they had told me in their private sessions. When they heard me describe honestly what had been so abundantly clear, the tension in the room went up significantly. Ultimately, they were waiting for "the man" and his reaction to my report. Until he spoke, from their perspective (as well as mine) all bets were off.

When Howard stood up, the tension was palpable. I was holding my breath, because I knew what he had to say, and I was praying for his sake that he had the wisdom—and the strength—to say it.

Howard looked the members of his management team straight in the eye, one by one, and then said the following: "I've listened very carefully to what David has said, and as we move forward with this information I only have one thing to say to you: Are you with me or are you against me?"

I was flabbergasted! You could feel the disappointment in the room. Looks of disgust and sadness were passed between the eyes of the 25 managers present. The chairman gave me a look I will never forget, and the meeting ended quickly, with that certain rumbling you hear as a train approaches in a dark tunnel.

But Howard then turned to me and said the most amazing thing. "I think that went well, don't you?" It was one of the few times in my career that I was speechless.

After 20 "productive" years at the hospital, Howard was gone in a week. To this day, he is still bitter and doesn't know what he did wrong. And to this day, I am convinced that his inability to say "I'm sorry" was the major factor in his downfall.

Ultimately, to say you are sorry takes deep courage. In my experience, even the worst of mistakes can be forgiven if you are willing to do three things.

First, you must apologize, with sincerity and without self-justification. An apology that says, "I'm sorry, but if you hadn't done this, I wouldn't have done that," is no apology at all.

Second, you should talk about what you've learned from the experience. This helps put the situation in a learning context and helps create empathy.

Finally, and most critically, you need to say what you will do differently in the future.

Of course, your credibility will only carry you so far if you establish a pattern of apology followed by another explosion. Eventually, you will lose all believability. You likely will be perceived as manipulative (which, in case you hadn't noticed, you probably are) and not to be trusted.

During times of change and the stress that comes with it, we often need to treat each other in a kinder and more forgiving manner. Tempers flare and emotional fuses get short when individuals or teams are under stress. It never ceases to impress me how the simple act of admitting fault can quickly help create a new beginning or deepen the intimacy that exists in the current relationship.

When going through change, ask yourself, "Where do I need to apologize for feelings I may have inadvertently hurt or for actions that may have caused harm?" Then rectify whatever you need to, using the three steps. You will be amazed at the positive impact it will have on your effectiveness with others.

KEEP YOUR EYES ON THE PRIZE

The main thing is to keep the
main thing the main thing.

—Unknown

Many years ago, while a graduate student traveling Ireland, I had an opportunity to have dinner with Mother Teresa. She was still Sister Teresa back then, and relatively unknown to the world. I was a poor graduate student given an opportunity by a kind-hearted priest to share a meal with a visiting nun. I knew nothing about her or her cause, but a free dinner was a free dinner. And so I went.

The evening was beautiful. Fifty people sat under a tent lit by the sun setting over the hills of western Ireland. For reasons that are still unknown to me, I was seated next to Mother Teresa.

To break the ice, we chatted about her work, her views of Indian poverty, and the politics of the church. She asked me about my life, the work I was doing, and my college career. Oddly enough (in retrospect), we traded a lot of jokes. Being Jewish, I didn't bring in the attitude of reverence for nuns that someone who'd grown up Catholic might naturally have. And, of course, I had no idea who Teresa was or who she would become in the eyes of the world. I was respectful, but curious, and I think she found my naiveté refreshing—in the way you might also find a class of fifth graders at career night refreshing! We had a delightful time.

Then the most remarkable thing happened. When the waitress arrived to serve dinner to Sister Teresa, the nun held up her hand to prevent her. "Excuse me," she said. "How much did that food cost?"

"Excuse me?" the bewildered waitress replied.

"I said, how much did that cost?"

"Uhhh. I don't know," the waitress responded.

"Then please find out."

The next thing I knew, the manager came running over in a panic. "Is there a problem?" she frantically asked.

"No," Teresa replied. "I just wanted to know how much my dinner cost."

"Uhhh. Why?" the manager asked.

"Because," Teresa calmly explained, "My people back in India can't use this food, so I want the money instead!"

"I don't understand," the poor manager replied.

Now in a very loud voice, so that everyone could hear, Sister Teresa clearly enunciated, "My people cannot eat this food. It does them no good. So I respectfully demand that you give me the money instead!"

You can imagine the uproar that ensued. Of course, she got her food *and* its equivalent in money (and a lot more money, too, from what I could tell).

Sister Teresa sent a very powerful directive that evening to all those present under that tent. Essentially, her message was this: There are things that matter, and things that don't. That lesson has never left me.

My grandmother said it another way: "You can have anything you want. You just can't have everything you want."

This principle of clear, consistent focus is vitally important in any organization. IBM adopted the following credo: "Better, faster, cheaper." Every decision is measured against this motto. If it doesn't fit the cause, then it gets sent to the back of the line.

Another great company, General Electric, with all the massive change initiatives it has gone through over the years, tries very hard to stick to the following credo: Never have more than three to five major initiatives going on at once. GE believes that a company—even a huge one—that has more than a chosen few priorities will be a house divided against itself. If everything is important, then, in truth, nothing is important.

I had a Fortune 50 client involved in a massive $130 million change effort. They would often use the expression "clear the decks" to signal to their 200 organizational leaders that this effort was a top priority. Unfortunately, they also had about 15 other efforts going on that frequently got the same "clear the decks" message. After a while, despite the best intentions, the company leadership became overstretched and vulnerable to confusion and cross-purposes. You can talk all you want about managing "multiple priorities," but the lack of organizational clarity left waters swirling around the deck of that ship.

One day, in an effort to suggest the problem, I gathered all 200 managers in a windowless room. I then asked them to close their eyes and point to true north. Of course, you can imagine the results. Fingers were pointed in every possible direction, including up and down. This was the truth of the organizational priorities they'd been given. When they opened their eyes, they all started laughing at the absurdity of their predicament.

Yes, our lives and our work are increasingly complex; yes, we often need to be able to manage multiple tasks. But people need to know, when push comes to shove, how to make the hard choices. Where do I put my time, energy, and resources when 20 voices are demanding 30 things? What does our organization regard as truly critical?

As a leader in your organization, you must be willing to support your managers when they justifiably choose not to engage in certain work because it is outside the parameters of the truly critical. Remember the question of Sister Teresa: "How much does it cost?" Test the value of every potential action to the larger whole. If it is not critical to your mission or your nature as a company—drop it.

GREAT LEADERS ARE INCLUSIVE, NOT EXCLUSIVE

We are not here to be successful.
We are here to be creative.

—The Upanishads

Most of us are not very good at handling conflict. Our tendency is either to duck it or to nuke it, depending on our style. Yet conflict is an inevitable part of any organizational life, and studies show that 90 percent of all conflicts are between people with long-term relationships. So if you hope to have any lasting relationships, conflict is part of the territory.

The good news is that conflict also can offer great opportunity. The cross-cultural anthropologist Angeles Arrien refers to conflict as "a call to our creative," an invitation to work in new and different ways, setting aside our fears and anxieties. Conflict is also a chance to practice behaviors that are inclusive rather than exclusive—to act in a way that brings people together and promotes healing rather than discord and distance.

Unfortunately, our natural tendency is the reverse. Because conflict means pain, we tend to move away from it rather than toward it, seeking ways, either subtle or direct, to distance ourselves either from the issue or individual. It takes a great leader to embrace conflict as a means of creating forward movement during change.

I learned this from my colleague Sandra Janoff, the coauthor of *Future Search* and a leading expert on collaborative change. She taught me that, in a group, when an individual voice of dissent is expressed, it is important to fight our natural tendency to ignore or refute it. When an angry voice declares, "This project is a loser!" many leaders will tend to respond by saying something like, "That's an interesting statement, Bob. Does anyone here have a different viewpoint?" It's a very subtle shift. While appearing attentive, the leader tries to move the spotlight off the dissent by enlisting support for his own point of view. The goal is to move away from the conflict and quietly shut down the dissident individual.

But this strategy rarely works. When we differ from our colleagues and do not feel heard, we'll usually continue to speak our mind. Most of us don't want to feel alone, so when we're isolated from our group, we'll want to repeat our message louder and more vociferously until we recruit some support.

So the consequence of exclusionary behavior is that those pushed away only become heightened in their own feelings. If you try to shut someone down, their sense of personal dignity will be hurt, and though they may say nothing at the time, their anger and pain will typically go into an emotional vault where it will sit, accumulating interest, until a later time when it can be withdrawn—often explosively.

So try moving against your instincts when an inflammatory statement is made. Take a deep breath and try to offer an inclusive response that joins with—agrees with—some part of the statement. Agreement in part does not mean that one agrees in whole. But it does mean that we do not leave a voice hanging out there alone, no matter what.

For example, try responding with, "Interesting perspective. Is there anything in what was said that someone can agree with?" Hear a few supportive comments, and only then shift to alternative points of view. Time and again I've seen contentious individuals start to shift their perspectives simply because they have been acknowledged. Sometimes that is all we want.

I truly believe that in any form of communication sits the same need—the desire to be heard and appreciated. Responding at that level, and only that level, can quickly shift contentious and ingrained perspectives.

The philosophy of moving toward conflict is a little like standing waist-deep in the ocean at the very place where the surf crashes. Our initial tendency is to grimace and brace ourselves against the force of the waves. But if we choose instead to dive into the breaking surf, we find we can move forward easily, with minimal struggle.

STAY GOSSIP-FREE

If you don't have anything nice to say
about anyone, come sit by me.

—Alice Longsworth Roosevelt

One of my favorite jokes is about how new members are initiated into a Jewish women's card group. As part of the introduction, each new member is informed of what is not discussed over cards: "We don't talk about our husbands, because they're all schmucks. And we don't talk about our furs, because they're all gorgeous. And we don't talk about our grandchildren, because they're all geniuses. And we don't talk about our sex lives, because what was, was!"

In every group, there are certain things that are simply not discussed.

As human beings, we have a natural tendency to want to be right, and in the quest for satisfaction of that desire we'll do almost anything. We'll gossip, collude, be indiscreet, and drag in other people to support our view. We'll take any subtle advantage to support our points, no matter how ultimately destructive our acts may be. Thus, at any given time in any organization, you will hear a multitude of indiscreet statements being made that undermine and sabotage the foundations of trust that are essential to successful transitions.

This is dangerous for two reasons. First, one should always beware of creating cliques and alliances during any transition, because things change. Those who are angry and not talking to each other today may find themselves sharing an office or project tomorrow. Politics may make strange bedfellows, but the bedposts frequently rotate. The Spanish have a saying, "Whoever gossips to you will gossip about you." I can't count the number of organizational transitions that I've seen in which formerly battling peers ended up reporting to one another. So keeping your behavior impeccable is an essential aid to corporate longevity.

The second reason is even more critical. All team dynamics, I'm sorry to say, inevitably take us back to the first group we were ever with—our family. Actions and behaviors that may seem irrational are often signs that individuals are working out their earlier family dynamics. Listen to the complaints of those around you: "I feel totally unappreciated." "That was *my* project!" "Why do *I* have to do it? That's Johnson's area!" If you compare these to the arguments our kids have at home, the patterns seem obvious.

Psychologists have been saying for years that this playing out of family dynamics is what ultimately keeps organizations from being effective. And I have yet to witness anything that proves them wrong. So during changing times, when those around the managing team are looking for stability, they begin to look toward the senior or executive team as representing the old parental alliance. During any change, we want to feel assured that Mom and Dad are on solid ground. This makes uncontrolled conflict especially painful and troubling.

It is certainly fine to argue behind closed doors, but once the team moves into the public venue, a game face should be adopted at all costs, so as to send a cohesive message. If it isn't, the team either will be open to outside manipulation or will risk increasing organizational anxiety substantially. After all, who wants to follow a group into battle that is battling among themselves?

So the best rule of thumb is, "Inside the room, all's fair. Outside the room, we keep a together face." To think that any leak won't spread like wildfire and get back to the person discussed is an exercise in wishful thinking. Gossip and bad news travel fast. Nothing will destroy trust on a team more quickly than to have an agreement of confidentiality broken. Nothing!

Private matters taken public only serve to create mistrust and fear. Where there is no safety, there is no trust. An example of this can be found in any small New Hampshire town that uses the selectman process to govern. In my home town of Peterborough, for example, we have three capable individuals elected by the public to serve as town leaders. These selectmen essentially play the role of either mayor or city council. The problem is that recently, in a well-intentioned attempt to create a spirit of openness and minimize any potential for shenanigans, the state instituted a so-called "right to know" law. The selectmen can never get together at any time for any reason (unless a very special exception is made) without it being open to the public and the press. They literally can't even have breakfast together without inviting reporters.

The impact is frequently awkward. Imagine if every issue, every personal problem in your team, could potentially get played out in the public eye. There would be no safety, no opportunity to make mistakes, no dignity. It is an extreme example, but the principle is the same.

The role of leadership is to manage the boundary between private and public as skillfully as possible. Remind yourself and your team of the importance of confidentiality, and discuss the issue (and potential lapses) on a frequent basis. The consistent violation of this principle is one of the few issues I support quick termination over.

KEEP A NEUTRAL EYE

The mind contains all possibilities.

—Jack Kornfield

Our perceptual framework, the way we frame our view of what's around us, is the sum of our learning, our experience, and our personal values. It's inevitable that we should develop such a framework, and it's a vital coping tool. Yet when we become so rigid in our framework that we cease to see other options, we often find ourselves in big trouble. Staying neutral is the way through. When we abandon neutrality, our ability to create new, positive alternatives can become seriously impaired.

Here's an example. A certain patient had a series of bad experiences with the nursing department at a medium-sized hospital in a close-knit rural community. The patient's daughter, upset over the treatment her mother had received, fired off a letter of complaint to the hospital president. Being both sensitive to customer relations and a believer in delegation, he handed the letter to the vice president of nursing and said, "Please take care of this."

This is where the story gets interesting. In some healthcare arenas, there's a cultural dynamic that says, "Nursing is taken for granted and is often under attack." This happened to be true at this organization. The VP of nursing immediately lost her neutrality and went into a mode of "I must defend my department." She was hooked, and could not see any option besides moving into a familiar pattern of attack and defense. The consequences were an amazing lesson in the need for detachment.

Knowing that the president was keen on service, and with all good intention, she launched into her response. The VP spent almost two weeks (at a salary of $140,000 per year) investigating the issues and writing a response in a point-by-point letter to the family, documenting that most of the patient's complaints were either misunderstandings or, in fact, the result of errors made by the family. When it was completed, she proudly brought her letter to the president for his review before sending it.

To say the least, he was less than pleased. "We have a customer service issue here," he said. "This is what I want. First, take your letter and rip it up. Then take $25 out of petty cash and go down to the gift shop and buy some flowers. Then get into your car, drive to this woman's house, apologize for any problems we may have caused to her and her family, and present the flowers. Then get back into your car, and return to work. That's how I want you to solve the problem!"

The VP was shocked. It was inconceivable to her that solving the problem in this particular way was even an option. All she saw was an issue that her department was going to get grief over. Her lack of neutrality only led to a solution that, more than likely, would have thrown gasoline on the fire.

Yes, it's true that we must investigate and document any complaints from customers. It is a critical part of any business environment, especially in today's tumultuous and overly litigious healthcare climate. But that is only part of the truth. If our fears lock us into a way of thinking that keeps us from seeing different options, a bigger price is paid.

When we get attuned to a particular perspective, when all we see is one possibility, we lock out creative alternatives that may more effectively resolve our problems.

Can you imagine in a small, rural community how many positive phone calls would have gone out after that visit from the VP? ("Harriet, it's me. Guess who just stopped over to bring me flowers? You'll never believe it!") Whether a personal visit (versus flowers and a letter) was the right thing to do is up for grabs. There are clearly tough realities in our litigious society. That is a hard truth.

But what's critical to remember is that by locking into a particular point of view, we close down our available options and choices. It is essential for us to track our limited thinking so during those times when a creative solution is called for we can rise to the occasion.

The next time you are feeling overwhelmed and boxed in by an issue, ask yourself how you might move to a neutral place. What attachments do you have regarding outcome or process that do not allow you to take a broader view? What alternatives can you seek to solve the problem in a new and different way?

When we lose our neutral eye, we also lose the ability to rise above the fray and see the wide range of solutions that are always there, if only we could see them.

CREATING CLARITY
THROUGH INSPIRATION

I'm desperately trying to figure out why
kamikaze pilots wear helmets.

—Dave Edison

In *Proceedings,* the magazine of the Naval Institute, Frank Koch tells this story. It is a classic because it so vividly clarifies what happens when we get lost in a view of the world:

Two battleships assigned to a training squadron had been at sea on maneuvers in heavy weather for several days. I was serving on the lead battleship and was on watch on the bridge as night fell. The visibility was poor with patchy fog, so the captain remained on the bridge keeping an eye on all activity.

Shortly after dark, the lookout on the wing of the bridge reported, "Light bearing off the starboard bow."

"Is it steady or moving astern?" the captain called out.

Lookout replied, "Steady, captain," which meant we were on a dangerous collision course with that ship.

The captain then called to the signal man, "Signal that ship: We are on a dangerous collision course, advise you change course 20 degrees."

Back came a signal, "Advisable for *you* to change course 20 degrees."

The captain said, "Send: I'm a captain, change course 20 degrees."

"I'm a seaman second class," came the reply. "*You* had better change course 20 degrees."

By this time the captain was furious. He spat out, "Send: I'm a battleship. Change course 20 degrees!"

Back came the flashing light. "I'm a lighthouse!"

We changed course.

The loss of neutrality puts at risk our ability to respond clearly. We lose our internal compass, which gives us the capacity to right ourselves when the world is changing fast. How does this happen?

When we change the rules, we fundamentally shift the internal support mechanisms that are the foundation of our behaviors and beliefs. Essentially, we lose the psychological foundations upon which we act and respond to the world. The world as we know it and believe it to be is suddenly a very different place.

Years ago I visited Hawaii's Kilauea volcano. It had been erupting in a slow stream of lava that poured into the ocean. At night, the sight of a red-river of molten rock hitting the water and the resultant mile-high tower of steam was spectacular. You could walk within a hundred yards of the flow and feel the heat on your face. I'll never forget the feeling of walking on brand-new, crunchy lava-formed earth that was warm to the touch like fresh-baked bread. In that moment, all I had believed about the Earth I walked on (especially that it was old—very, very old) shifted as I now walked on land that was newer than I was. It was both exhilarating and a little disturbing. It's a common feeling among people who experience an earthquake for the first time.

A large organizational change can have the same effect on us. Like an earthquake or volcano, it can rattle us to the core, leaving us with little to hold on to or believe. Staying neutral is not even an option. We become awash in fear and uncertainty. When this occurs, we must find a new form of stability and root the psyche in something new and different.

What that means is we must create patterns of thinking that will support new ways of being—new internal qualities that will help us move beyond our old habits and behaviors. This is the good fight—a battle of the old fears and the resultant confusion against the new hopes and the clarity they can bring.

In this struggle for clarity, it is critical to understand that we are always, as anthropologist Angeles Arrien says, "bigger than our patterns." Ultimately, our core character is larger and more expansive than our fears, self-doubts, and insecurities. The task at hand is to find something that will pull us through the uncertainty.

The key—what enables great leaders to guide others through change, tragedy, and turmoil—is inspiration. Inspiration is a powerful tool to manage the complexity that comes through the hardship of change. General George Patton, Microsoft chairman Bill Gates, and servant of the poor Mother Teresa, are about as different from one another as you could imagine. And yet in their leadership they all had one thing in common: They were all inspired by the focus of their work and the clarity of their vision.

Joseph Campbell, the brilliant scholar, said it another way: "Follow your bliss." If you can find inspiration in the heat of the change, no matter where, then that will both strengthen your character against your fears and create clarity out of confusion. I have a client who calls it, "finding the irresistible proposition."

What is your irresistible proposition? Where are you inspired? What do you need to do to bring forward more of that inspired voice in your place of work? Have recent changes dampened your sense of aliveness, so that you are now a member of the walking dead?

Among certain indigenous cultures, if you were depressed or feeling out of balance, they would call it "soul loss." As a means of seeking help, you would often go to your medicine man or shaman, who as a form of diagnosis would ask the following four questions: "When in your life did you stop singing? When in your life did you stop dancing? When in your life did you stop being enchanted with your own life's story? And when in your life did you stop feeling comfortable with the sweet territory of silence?" By pondering the answers to these four questions, you could often return to a place of clarity and balance. Essentially, what was being asked was, when did you stop being inspired?

To return to that place of inspiration and find what you need to right your internal ship often requires nothing more than listening to the internal voice of wisdom that is always present. We think it is hard, because all we feel is the confusion that comes from fear and uncertainty. It's not. It requires a little patience, some quiet, and the willingness to listen to the answers.

Your assignment? For one month, find a quiet spot to sit for 15 minutes a day. That's it. Close your eyes and ask yourself the question, "Where am I inspired?" Then don't do anything. Just sit and wait for the answer. Be patient. This is not about doing anything or creating anything. It is about listening to the internal voice that truly knows what we want and need. If you are diligent and disciplined, you will get your answer.

The clarity that inspiration provides can be both a lifesaver for you and a lighthouse beacon for others.

STAY OUT OF THE MIDDLE

Between what I think I want to say,
what I believe I'm saying, what I say,
what you want to hear, what you
believe you understand and what
you understood, there are at least
nine possibilities for misunderstanding.

—François Garagnon

If you're a leader, you must do your best to stay neutral during internal conflicts on your team. The ultimate goal is to play what is sometimes referred to among traditional societies as the role of the "fair witness"—the uninvolved observer who sits above the issues and manages the conflicts to successful resolution. Yes, I know—it's very easy to get sucked in; very seductive, in fact.

One of the concerns most frequently voiced to me by senior executives is, "I keep getting put in the middle. I wish my people would solve their problems themselves." When I suggest the need to stay out of the middle, what I often hear is, "If they have a problem, then guess who else has a problem? Me! So I feel compelled to help fix it because it makes my job easier." In the short term, maybe. In the long term, no. Being in the middle, as the apex of a triangle of conflict, will inevitably set team

members against each other, encouraging indirect communication and dependence on you as the intermediary.

You must be watchful for very subtle forms of this tri-
angulation, the goal of which is to get you to collude with
a particular point of view and support one person against
another. The ploys people use can be exquisitely elegant.
A conversation might begin with an innocent, "Jane? I
could really use your advice on how to handle a situation
that has come up," followed by a covert attempt to persuade you to a particular point of view. The politics of
win-lose are now in motion, with your favor as the ultimate prize.

That doesn't mean, of course, that you must never
offer your opinion or make decisions that affect others.
However, the question you need to ask when placed in
the middle is, "What is the intention here?" If it feels a little murky, or if you sense that an individual is trying to use
you as leverage, then a power play is in motion, and mis-
chief is usually afoot. Trust your internal radar. It will
serve you well. Leaders who trust the warning signs are
rarely led off base.

It's a familiar problem from nonwork settings, of
course. In my immediate family, the use of third-party
involvement to resolve conflict has been a long and painful norm. If my mother is upset at my sister, she won't
speak directly to her about it. Instead, she'll tell my other
sister, who will tell my brother, who will tell me—because
I am close to the sister in trouble and maybe will talk to

her. By the time all is said and done, we have a mess on our hands. It is crazy-making.

A while ago, I decided to take myself out of the role of family diplomat. I instituted a new family policy: If you come to me about a conflict with another family member, and it is clear that the two members in conflict have not spoken to one another, I do not want to hear about it. If you are coming to me for advice (i.e. "How would you deal with so and so?"), then I will listen with this understanding. But you must speak to the person with whom you have a conflict within 24 hours and get back to me and let me know how it went. If I don't hear from you in a week, then my coaching days on this issue are over. Plain and simple.

How well does this really work? Truth be told, I do my best. But it's my family. The pressure gets intense, and sometimes I get caught in the seduction of family gossip. However, due to my attempt at norm-breaking behavior, the family environment is much improved, and I am less entangled in what I believe are unhealthy dynamics.

What's interesting is that I've suggested the same policy to my consulting clients, and they love it. Somehow, clarifying specific norms about a problem that we all know erodes the integrity of our organizational "families" is very helpful. Will it be an easy change to make? Probably not. This pattern is an old one, and for most people, an early one. At first, you probably won't be believed when you let others know about the new rules of engagement. Then you will be tested. Then they'll get pissed ("If you really cared about me, you'd listen!"). But essentially these responses are all forms of resistance to being responsible for managing their own conflicts in an honest and up-front manner.

Make a change here, and you will improve your team's integrity in a real and meaningful way.

TRUST YOUR INSTINCTS

Regret for the things we did can be tempered by time; it is regret for the things we did not do that is inconsolable.

—Sydney Harris

The story of how my parents met is an amazing and inspirational one. They were both first-generation Americans, their parents eastern European Jews who'd emigrated in the early 1900s to New York City. My father's family settled in the Bronx, my mother's in Brooklyn: two boroughs in the same city, but worlds apart. It was, as they say, a mixed marriage: one family rooted for the Brooklyn Dodgers, the other for the New York Yankees.

They met in 1950, in Miami Beach. They'd both gone down there for a spring vacation with friends. While my father was a bit more traveled, it was my mother's first time out of the state, besides a few trips to New Jersey. She was 18 and seen by her parents as a golden, naïve beauty, not quite ready to enter the reality of the hard, outside world.

They met on a Thursday in an elevator. They started talking and fell madly in love. After that, they spent every free minute they could together, and my father proposed the following Sunday—four days later! Even more amazingly, my mother said, "Yes!" Imagine committing to marriage (at a time when divorce was not really an option) after only four days. I won't buy a new car until I've researched and thought about it for at least a year.

When they returned from their one-week vacation in Florida and announced the news to their families, it was not well received. But my father first went to Brooklyn, where he spoke eloquently to my mother's parents about his love and his intentions. They were more Americanized than my other grandparents and had a deeper understanding of the ways of the new country. Her parents were impressed by his passion, and he was given the seal of approval.

My mother then had to make the long trip to the Bronx to meet her future in-laws. My father's parents were much more old-fashioned, speaking in thick Jewish accents and staying within a closed circle of friends and family. They were very protective of their son and terribly upset at the recent turn of events. It was way out of their frame of understanding, and they were not happy.

They lived in a small tenement apartment in a fourth-floor walk-up. With great anxiety, my mother rang the doorbell and waited for what was sure to be a less-than-pleasant welcome. She was not disappointed. My grandmother, who was once described as "about as warm as a pickle" (whatever that means), answered the door and said coolly, "Welcome, Bernice. Please follow me." She led my mother into the living room, where all the furniture had been cleared away. The room was empty except for 22 chairs placed in a circle, in which all of my father's relatives sat, glum and silent. Within the circle sat one empty chair, which my mother was then directed to take by my grandmother. She was about to be tested.

Without fanfare, my grandmother began. "Now, Bernice. Before you should marry our boy Stanley, we of his family have two questions we would like to ask. The first question is, 'What do you want from the family?' And the second question is, 'What are you willing to give to the family?'"

My mother, like my father, also spoke very lovingly and eloquently. She talked about family, love, kindness, and commitment. She left accepted and approved. In truth, though not set up very supportively, the ordeal-by-interview was a brilliant opportunity for her—and she handled it beautifully.

My parents ended up having a very happy, committed, magical relationship, until my father's untimely death 19 years later.

This story is a wonderful lesson in the value of trust, of seeing what you want and pursuing it, regardless of contrary voices. Sometimes those voices are internal ones that wear the face of reality. They are often born of fear and concern, and speak a need to maintain the status quo. After all, who would agree to marry after only four days? It's unheard of.

Often the voices are external ones, wanting to know what the trade-offs will be and insisting that your ideas make no sense. Imagine the courage of my mother as an 18-year-old to trust her vision against the emotional on-slaught of 22 future in-laws.

The ability to pursue your dream no matter what may be the most important quality needed for managing change. It requires courage and conviction of spirit to weather the hard times. To fully commit to the vision we hold, we must trust ourselves at a deep instinctual level. If we don't, then we will never conquer the internal or exter-nal voices of doubt that decry every difficult transition.

All great leaders and entrepreneurs speak of the need to hold fast to the image of the possible. It means listen-ing to what scholar Joseph Campbell calls "your trajec-tory." It is a deep personal image, as individual as a thumb print, that makes your leadership both unique and com-pelling to others. No one else in the world will ever man-age a situation in exactly the same way as you will; no problem will ever be handled in quite the same manner as you will handle it; no one else dreams exactly the same as you do. Ultimately, this is what makes management an art, not a science.

Campbell writes, "When the world seems to be falling apart, stick to your own trajectory; hang onto your own ideals and find kindred spirits. That's the rule of life. Spengler has an image of the ideal when all's falling apart; he says it's the soldier in Pompeii who stayed right at his post when the volcanic ash was coming down. Even at the worst moment, if you are holding on to your trajectory, you've won. It's those who get thrown off track who are lost."

In my work, I am often called on to help solve thorny organizational problems. I can sit with leaders for hours, tossing around possible solutions to complex conundrums. Yet sometimes no amount of discussion will clarify the issue. In such moments of confusion, I have learned that the best question to ask is, "What does your gut tell you?"

During times of difficulty, find a quiet place and settle in for a while. Listen to some music. Take a walk. Stare out a window. Do nothing. Try to tap the wellspring of internal wisdom that always exists, and, after a while ask, "What do my instincts tell me?" The easiest part of the process is the asking. The hardest part is to really listen and act on the answer. If you've done your homework— if you've really worked the issue and still cannot decide the best course of action—then the instinctual response will almost always be the best one. Listen to that voice, and then have the courage to move accordingly.

The great mystic poet Rumi once wrote, "Move from within. Do not let fear move you the way it wants to. Begin a foolish project. Noah did!" So did my parents; so does every great adventurer or dreamer.

FISH IN MUDDY WATERS

There's more good than evil in the world . . . but not by much.

—Zalman Schacter

Wilma Mankiller, a great contemporary Native American leader, wears a choker that has the faces of two wolves on it. A reporter once asked her what they stood for. "This one," she said, pointing to one face, "represents the voice of good. And this one represents the voice of evil. They are always in battle."

"Which one is winning?" the reporter asked.

Her response was quite profound: "The one I feed the most."

The shadow of fear is an unfortunate part of many organizational cultures. In New York, for instance, the world of finance is basically predicated on one philosophy—produce or be fired. All behaviors short of flagrantly breaking the law are tolerated if you are making money.

Al Dunlap, a.k.a. "Chainsaw Al," the former CEO of Scott Paper and Sunbeam, is another example. Before his fall from grace, he used a "scorched earth" policy to manage change, firing employees by the thousands, cutting costs heedlessly, and even driving the remaining workers mercilessly. What is unfortunate is not the rarity but the familiarity of this style. We are becoming a country where strategic planning that involves others and considers the human impact is readily sacrificed for short-term results.

This is a myopic view, one that succumbs to our fears rather than our values.

If your strategy is to manage change using fear, your people will become like fish in muddy waters, no longer able to survive in the clear water of productivity. You will lose creativity, collaboration, and the ability to risk and change.

Fear has its place on a short-term basis, as in "If we don't work hard this quarter, we will lose our customer base." But in the process of change, long-term fear is rarely a reason that people will act with clarity and commitment.

In the late 1980s and early 1990s, I had a software client that produced medical management systems. Within 15 years, the company had grown exponentially from a small garage business to a leader in its industry. Catching the wave of medical information, it was in front of its limited competition and rode its success for all it was worth. The demand and need for its product was so high, the company couldn't help but make money—lots and lots of money.

The CEO was tough and distant. He would grunt and snort through his day like a rampaging bull. His meetings were infamous for the heads that rolled and the careers that were lost on single small mistakes. His favorite saying was, "The two best motivators are fear and hunger!"

When he walked the halls of his growing company, the impact was profound. People parted in his path as if he were Moses crossing the Red Sea—not out of respect, but for self-preservation. They were sacred to death of him.

As the industry started to change from external competition, technological innovation, and industry regulation, the need for creative, clear thinking was becoming essential. The company needed bright, fresh products that would maintain its innovative image.

But no one—not a single member of the senior or management team—would willingly bring forward any ideas that either weren't safe or conservative. The ability to make quantum jumps in thinking had never been fostered, because fear usually produces the need for self-preservation. And self-preservation rarely leads to breakthroughs, because it is safety based.

Today, in a highly competitive marketplace, the company is foundering. It has lost its niche, position, and market share. Its stock has plummeted. Takeover or acquisition rumors are rampant, and the company is in deep, deep trouble.

Look in the mirror. What do you want to create? What is your core value? Like Wilma Mankiller, we always have a choice. Which wolf do you feed the most?

LISTEN FOR THE DANGEROUS TRUTH

It may be that your sole purpose in life
is to serve as a warning to others.

—Unknown

In my experience, all companies, even great ones, at some point are faced with a dangerous truth. It may come in the guise of a subtle suspicion or a faint pattern that foreshadows a market change or a significant operational flaw. The only way to deal with this kind of critical information is with an unrelenting dedication to the truth without concern for the status quo or personal ego. Almost every company will make critical mistakes in its history, either through misguided action or ill-conceived inaction. But the great business debacles, from the failure of U.S. auto makers in the 1970s to anticipate the rise of the imports to Apple's near-fatal loss of market share in the 1990s, have been caused by an unwillingness to proactively deal with the dangerous truth when the early warning signs were present.

I'm currently involved in a turnaround situation with a publicly held company that enjoyed an early, meteoric success. Yet from the start, there were certain key operational weaknesses that threatened the organizational infrastructure. As a result, the company was getting to the point where it could no longer deliver the product it was selling. Everyone in the back office knew there was a big problem, but the leadership chose not to surface the issue for discussion. While the leaders were riding a wave of optimism that came from earlier successes, the momentum for disaster was building back on shore. Finally, in one very bad day, the stock collapsed from $80 a share to $20 in a little over two hours.

One key executive, who personally lost $60 million that day, told me later, "We could have seen it coming, but we chose to ignore the inevitable because we were doing so well. We didn't want to challenge the status quo. We were successful, and who could argue with that?"

What keeps this kind of crucial yet hidden information from emerging so it can be dealt with and managed? The answer often lies in what my friend and colleague Rod Napier calls "the seduction of the executive." Napier has spent a lifetime coaching senior executive teams, and his premise is both simple and alarming. He believes that information often doesn't travel upstream within organizational hierarchies because senior leadership sends out subtle messages that it wants only positive news. This is reinforced in two ways. First, and most obviously, you kill the messenger—a long-standing practice since the days of ancient Rome. The second form of reinforcement is more subtle: The work is so much fun, the business is so successful, and the president is so nice that no one wants to ruin things by bearing bad news.

The latter was the case with my turnaround client. During the company's glory days, everyone was making a lot of money, having a great time, and working for a terrific guy. The seduction occurred when the people who needed objective information to guide the company forward were receiving less than adequate data. No one wanted to risk being seen as the one who killed the golden goose. The organization had people who knew the truth—but they wouldn't bring it forward! By the time the harsh marketplace finally told the emperor he had no clothes, the fall was swift and painful.

The written Chinese symbol for crisis is composed of the two interlinked characters of danger and opportunity. When the opportunity for change presents itself, make sure you're vigilant in seeking out hidden dangerous truths that may be present. Watch out for your own seduction patterns and keep asking, "If we were to make one critical mistake, what would it be?" Ask this question a lot and ask it often of as many different people in as many levels in your organization as possible. Do not expect the information to come easily. But when it does, don't hesitate to act accordingly.

MANAGE THE TENSION

We are trying to teach our people how
to fly an airplane when they don't know
how to get to the airport.

—Frank Glaviano

One Friday last year, I was flying out of National Airport in Washington, D.C., to my home in New Hampshire. Waiting in the departure lounge were the plane's passengers, an assortment of businesspeople, families, and older adults, all tired, road-weary, and ready to go home. Then the announcement came: our plane would be two hours late; the new expected arrival time would be 9:35 P.M. This was critical, because National Airport has a 10:00 P.M. curfew. If the plane does not pull away from its gate at 10:00 P.M., you have to come back the next day; no planes leave after curfew. You can imagine how delighted we all were at the possibility of an unplanned night's stay in our nation's capital. The collective groan could be heard three gates away.

Our gate manager, however, was an old hand, and as the time approached, he lined us up numerically by seat and row, with our bags ready to go. "Listen," he said. "The choice is yours. If you help each other out and move quickly, you can probably make it. If not, I'll see you tomorrow. It's up to you. The plane must be away from the gate at 10:00—not 10:01. The rules are very strict. So move fast, and watch out for your neighbor."

By 9:40, we were lined up on the walkway, and our plane pulled in. At 9:50, the plane had been emptied of its previous load of passengers, and we were ready to board. As I checked my watch and drew on hundreds of previous flight boardings as experience, I knew our situation was hopeless. We had a full flight with strollers, kids, an old lady with a walker, and lots of luggage. I was already preparing a call to my wife, who was not going to be happy. With just under ten minutes to go, we started our boarding attempt with a final word of encouragement from our gate manager, who reminded us that it could be done, if we helped each other. Think positive, he said, and remember your goal. "Right," I thought sardonically, "What have you been smoking?" However, just for laughs, I started the stopwatch function on my wrist-watch as the stampede began.

What followed was nothing short of miraculous. People flew down the aisles. Two college students carried the old lady. Those who had light burdens assisted other, overwhelmed travelers. I grabbed a stroller. Everyone kept asking, "How can I assist you?" The air was thick with shouts of "Help her out," and "Give him a hand." Before we knew it, we were all in our seats cheering and imploring the pilot to get going. When I checked my watch, I couldn't believe it. It had taken us seven minutes and 58 seconds to get everyone seated, with luggage stored and seat belts buckled. We had a full two minutes to spare!

What made this possible? Never underestimate the magic of a shared vision with shared benefits. But in order to create this kind of magic, every organizational leader must manage the creative tensions that are always present.

My colleague Cris Cappy uses a simple but brilliant metaphor when talking about managing change.

When a rubber band is pulled tight, as you might do when shooting it across the room, it represents the appropriate amount of creative tension that's needed to produce momentum and change. One side represents your current reality, the other side your compelling vision. Your organization will fail to move when you lack either one—the compelling vision or the clear sense of your current reality. Similarly, a rubber band will not spring from your hand if either the front end or back end is hanging loose. It must be taut enough to provide energy for movement, without being stretched so tight that it breaks. When the tension is right, it will create the energy for movement.

The role of leadership is to consistently balance the present truths of the environment with the sense of possibility that can come only from a compelling vision. Without a clear understanding of what's so, you will be building your castles on sand.

Likewise, without a clearly articulated vision with shared benefits, there is no reason to move quickly or with enthusiasm. When the organization is without a common direction, then the ability to galvanize energy is missing.

In my amazing adventure at National Airport, we all knew the reality of our situation, and what would happen if we didn't behave in atypical fashion. We also had a very clear, shared vision of a compelling and beneficial goal—to get home! The understanding of these two polarities allowed for action that was way outside of our realm of experience. Truthfully, it was a modern miracle.

As you move your organization forward, continue to make sure you and others know the reality of your environment. What are the truths that everyone needs to know? Where do you as an organization need to educate yourselves about the internal and external state of your business? Make sure as many of your people as possible know this.

Balance this with a shared understanding of the compelling vision. Do people want to go there? Does it excite them? Are you excited? Do you show it? Unless you can engage others around something they want, then it will be like trying to shoot a rubber band with no tension. It will drop at your feet.

LOOK FOR
STRATEGIC ALLIANCES

**When two bull elephants fight,
it is the grass that suffers.**

—African proverb

The following incident occurred in New Hampshire, where I live. The day after the ice storm of 1998, two people were attempting to make it to work. However, trees were down all over the roads, and the process was uncertain at best. One person was driving east and the other west, when they were both stopped in the middle of the highway by a large tree that had fallen, blocking traffic completely in both directions.

They both got out of their cars to survey the problem and do what New Englanders do best—trade stories about the weather. After a few minutes, they discovered that each worked in the other's hometown and that the road was clear to both their destinations except for the spot at which they now stood. Using Yankee ingenuity, they then took the only possible action to solve their problem—they swapped cars! They agreed to meet at 5:00 P.M. at the same spot and return the vehicles. Sure enough, at exactly five, they arrived at the still-blocked road and returned each other's automobiles. Their plan worked to perfection.

It's amazing to see what strategic alliances can accomplish when there's mutual urgency. Shared need is the best cement for relationships going through change. Just as at the heart of every conflict exist diametrically opposed desires, so the secret to negotiating effective alliances is to find areas of common need to build on.

A wonderful example of this occurred when Henry Kissinger, at that time the U.S. Secretary of State, met the Communist Chinese leader Mao Tse-Tung for the first time. During dinner, Mao leaned over and asked Kissinger what the United States wanted from China. Kissinger, always the diplomat, responded, "Nothing, sir, but your friendship."

"Nonsense," replied Mao. "You wouldn't have come if you didn't want something from us, and I wouldn't have offered an invitation if I didn't want something from you." With that shared recognition, real discussions between the two nations could begin.

I once had as a client a billion-dollar company in crisis. At the heart of the company's problem was the fact that the senior vice president of sales and the chief operating officer were constantly at odds. no matter how much the president tried to get them to "play nice," they continued to badmouth and sabotage one another. Their tension was dragging the rest of the company into chaos. Any attempts to discuss what was wrong and how to fix it disintegrated into name-calling and finger-pointing. It was a mess.

I was called in to conduct discussions between the two warring parties. It was immediately clear that they flat-out didn't like each other. No amount of holding hands and talking feelings would change their personal animosity toward each other. It was also clear that the president was loath to fire either party. The company was in a delicate turnaround situation, needing a strong short-term performance to bolster the stock price and increase immediate fiscal growth. Keeping both men on board rather than courting a major upheaval—as a dramatic firing would have done—was the option that had to work.

So it was clear that the goal of these meetings was to establish not a close friendship but a working détente between two challenging personalities. Under the circumstances, focusing on what had gone wrong would be a dead-end street. Instead, we urged them to focus their attention exclusively on what each wanted for the future. At first, they danced around direct questions like boxers sizing each other up in a ring. But as I continued to focus directly on their personal needs, it was clear that there was one thing they both wanted—to make a lot of money by selling the company. If the stock price rose 30 to 40 percent and the company became an acquisition target, both executives stood to become wealthy.

While this may sound obvious, it had eluded them completely up until this point. They were so engrossed in finger-pointing and being seen as "right" that they'd failed to consider what they would both gain from working together. It didn't take long for the lights to go on and for their self-interests to take hold. Today, while they are not the best of friends, they are at least civil to one another, and they start every private meeting by talking about how they will spend the next chapter of their lives—and all the wealth they expect to enjoy. A critical strategic alliance was struck by focusing exclusively and continuously on self-interest.

People are rarely at their best during change. The stress often brings out the worst in our personalities and character; we can become petty, anxious, and irrational, just when we need to be most focused and positive. During such moments, when alliances and teamwork are essential success factors, a straight-ahead focus on benefit will often bring warring parties together at the table.

EMBRACE THE UNKNOWN

The map is not the territory.

—Unknown

James Utterback, in his book *Mastering the Dynamics of Innovation,* tells the story of the American ice industry in New England in the late 1800s. It was a thriving business. Companies would cut ice from frozen lakes and sell them around the world. In one instance, Utterback writes:

"The largest single shipment was 200 tons that was shipped to India. One hundred tons got there unmelted, but this was enough to make a profit."

But innovation brought with it change. The ice harvesters were put out of business by those companies who invented mechanical ice makers. Thus, shipping was no longer an issue. You could make the ice in the city where it was needed.

These ice makers, however, were put out of business by companies who invented refrigeration. Why buy ice when you could make it in your own home?

The sad thing was the ice harvesters could never see the advantages of the new technology of ice making when it came to market. They continued to try and survive by doing what had always made them successful: better saws, better storage, better transportation. The ice makers in turn could never see the advantages of refrigerators and adopt this new technology to their business model. Neither the ice harvesters nor ice makers had the vision or capacity to see beyond what was known and successful to them at the time.

There is a term in psychology for this way of thinking. It is called *premature cognitive commitment*. It means humans will typically only act on what the memory of their past experience has taught them. Essentially, we limit ourselves by relying only on what we know. Our past limits our ability to change in the future.

A simple example is this: Take a jar, fill it with flies, and put a lid on it for a few days. When you take the lid off, very few of the flies will leave the jar. Their memory of what is possible and their experience limits their thinking and actions. Only the boldest of flies will leave the container that serves as an artificial boundary.

The business world is filled with examples of once-thriving industries that never changed their status quo, even once the writing was on the wall. In 1960, the Swiss controlled between 85 and 90 percent of the world market in wristwatches. Swiss watchmakers had a fine reputation for quality and reliability, and their timepieces were in demand everywhere.

Sometime in the 1960s, two Swiss engineers developed the world's first digital watch. A great technological breakthrough, you might think; but the engineers could find no interest in their own country in pursuing this new development. Try as they might, all doors remained closed. The repeated answer: "This digital toy will never replace the quality of a handmade Swiss timepiece. No one wants this!"

After much frustration, the engineers ended up selling their invention at an industry convention to two companies—Texas Instruments in the United States and Seiko Watches in Japan. Twenty years later, the Swiss watchmakers controlled only 8 percent of the world market. They'd denied the signs of onrushing change and paid the price for their blindness.

The question is, how can we learn to see beyond our boundaries and embrace unknown ideas? One answer may lie in a centuries-old tradition from the American Southwest.

The Mescalero Apache are famous around the world for their invisibility. They can seemingly blend into any environment and become unseen by the enemy, using minimal camouflage and trickery. Many accounts have been written of whole regiments of U.S. soldiers riding a few feet away from an Apache warrior without observing him—out in the open and yet unseen.

A number of years ago, I had an opportunity to spend some time with a Mescalero Apache elder who told me his tribe's secret. "We move in the negative space," he said.

"I don't understand."

"Look over there," he said, pointing to a grove of pinion pine. "What do you see?"

"I see some trees, some rocks, some scrub brush."

"Yes," he answered, "But what do you see *between* the trees, the rocks, and the brush?"

"Between . . . ?" I asked, perplexed.

"Yes, between. We rarely take note of the space that exists between objects. What do you see there?"

"Why, nothing. It's sort of an empty space that just exists. It's created by the space taken up by other things. I never took note of it before."

"Exactly! That is called 'negative space,' and it is where the Apache moves when he doesn't want to be seen. That is the secret of our invisibility. We stay in the negative space where we are never noticed."

"Well, then, how do I too learn to be invisible? To move in the negative space?" I urgently asked.

He quietly responded, "The first thing to remember is, it is always there."

Like the Apache warrior, we must remember that new ideas, approaches, and perspectives are always there. The secret is to constantly challenge yourself to see the unseen, the unknown on a daily basis. The gift of change is that it shakes up our current view of the world, better allowing us to see any negative space that exists. When we can do that then we can embrace the unknown.

The reason the New England ice manufacturers and the Swiss watch industry were so blind to change was because all they saw was the known world. They could not see between their perceptions to the negative space, the unknown potential. Like the soldiers, they passed by what they were seeking, and it was there all the time.

Every day, take a few minutes to look around your organization as if scanning unfamiliar terrain. What are people doing? How are they interacting? What products are manufactured or services conducted? You should know these answers. But now look for the negative space. What unknown, unseen potential exists between the cracks that could give you and your new organization a competitive advantage? If you do this every day, your ability to move through a changing environment with effective success will become greater, like that of the Apache in the wild.

PERFORMANCE BUYS FREEDOM

Why does Sea World have a seafood restaurant? I'm halfway through my fish burger and I realize "Oh my God . . . I could be eating a slow learner."

—Lynda Montgomery

A client of mine, John Broderick, director of sales training with Subaru of America, told me the following story a number of years ago. As John was growing up, his father had a classic old MG sports car. However, his father, being a "big man," literally outgrew the small interior of his automobile. He could no longer fit into his pride and joy. Instead of selling it, he emptied the fluids, covered it with a cloth, and stored it in the garage.

John was about 12 when this happened. When he turned 15, the obvious occurred to him: "Maybe this car could be mine!" You could not imagine a cooler car for a teenage male. So he started dropping hints to his dad on a weekly basis about the car: "If you're not doing anything with it, maybe I could have it. I mean, after all, it would be a shame to let such a beautiful car go to waste, and because I need a car, wouldn't this be the perfect solution? And it wouldn't cost anything. What do you think, Dad?"

His father never said a word. He would just let John ramble on and on without interrupting. No hint of what his plans or intentions for the car were. He'd end the conversation by saying simply, "I'll think about it."

On John's 16th birthday, his father took him to the garage and said the following: "Here are the keys to the MG. You are to take care of it for one year. You may drive it up and down the driveway, but not into the street. You may wash it, wax it, and change the oil, but for one year you are to drive the family station wagon. If you can drive the family car perfectly for one year, then on your 17th birthday the MG is yours, with no strings attached. But—and I mean this!—if you get one ticket, no matter how small, or if you're in one accident, regardless of who's at fault, I'll sell the MG the next day!"

John was thrilled. And you cannot imagine a more responsible, attentive new driver. The first year for any new driver is usually the most dangerous, but for John it was a year of intense safety awareness. He'd pull up to a stop sign, look left, look right, then look left again, and just to be sure, look right one more time before going ahead. He carried around $10 in quarters under the seat for parking meters. He never partied and drove. He was the model of decorum and responsibility—quite unheard of for a 16-year-old boy, brimming with hormones.

I am happy to report that, at 17, with a perfect driving record in hand, John was handed the keys to his dream car. It was a moment of accomplishment that he still talks about to this day. What's so wonderful about this story is that John knew exactly what he needed to do to be successful, and as long as he managed his performance effectively, he would be rewarded.

Another client of mine, Paul Sullivan, general manager of Shell Oil, uses the motto, "Performance buys freedom." The more his people perform, the less attention he gives them and the more individual autonomy they get. Paul relates it to his children. "When my kids are bringing home As on their report cards, I don't check their homework. But if their grades start to drop, I check it every night."

During changing times, it is important to carefully monitor the performance of your people and be crystal-clear about what will and will not bring your supervision. Arguably, it's a fine line between support and nagging. But Paul Sullivan's "homework model" provides a good clue. Manage your expectations around performance only, and let your people know this going in. If they are performing well, then give them autonomy. But if you see a drop in quality or productivity, then the ensuing tightness in management should be neither a surprise nor should it be resented.

Another client calls it, "Rewarding for performance and educating for failure."

VULNERABILITY BUILDS SUPPORT

I have always relied on the
kindness of strangers.

—Blanche DuBois in *A Streetcar Named Desire,*
by Tennessee Williams

In January of 1999, I went to Peru on vacation. I received rather hard news my first day. While walking down the street in Lima, I started to get severe chest pains. Talk about shock—one minute I was laughing and talking about erotic pottery, and the next I was doubled over, clutching at my chest.

An emergency physician and cardiologist saw me in a Lima hospital. After hooking me up to an EKG that looked like it came from the 1900s, he managed to say just two words in English: "Go home!"

Having been in Peru for just two days, I was on the next flight back, carrying nothing but a lot of fear.

After getting examined in the States, I was told I hadn't had a heart attack, but I did need a quintuple bypass operation. So on January 27th, at the age of 43, I went in for open-heart surgery.

Needless to say, I was shaken. A mere six months later, I was doing great, and as I became separated from my surgery, I began to see the incident for what it was—an amazing gift. Studies show that one in ten people with coronary blockage like mine suffer just the warning sign of angina, while five in ten have a heart attack, and the remaining four in ten drop dead. Why I suffered chest pains out of the blue one day at sea level, not the next day at 15,000 feet in a remote location where the consequences would have been dire, remains both a mystery and source of inspiration to me.

Buddhist teacher Jack Kornfield, once wrote, "Karma can change like the swish of a horse's tail." Everything I am writing about in this book organizationally I've experienced on a personal level. Of the many lessons I learned from my illness, I was most touched by the discovery that vulnerability brings support. It was the one learning that most deeply restored my faith in the human spirit and the kindness of others. We live in a cynical world and these are cynical times. But following my surgery I was reminded time and time again that maybe the world is a bit kinder than I believed it was.

While I received many kindnesses from friends and neighbors, it was the gestures from strangers that touched me most deeply. I found that opening myself in a vulnerable manner allowed others to move toward me in surprising and generous ways.

Here is my favorite example: I received exceptional care at my hospital, Catholic Medical Center in Manchester, New Hampshire. After I returned home, I decided to send a thank-you to the nurses on the Cardiac Unit in the form of five pizzas for lunch. I called the Domino's located near the hospital, and the manager, Michael Ives, answered the phone. I explained what I wanted, and more important why I wanted to send the pizzas. I described my condition and recent history. I wanted him to be very clear as to the gratitude this small token was intended to convey.

When it came time to give my credit card number for payment, Mr. Ives informed me that for payment he needed to swipe the actual credit card, and because I was no longer in the hospital this was not possible. When I told him I couldn't come in personally, he said he understood— and that the pizza and the delivery were on Domino's!

I was floored. To have this act of kindness and generosity bestowed by an unknown voice from a pizza company was very touching. I realize we're only talking about five pizzas, but that simple gesture has continued to stay with me to this day. Beyond the gift itself, I think I was most moved by the manager's warm, friendly, and matter-of-fact tone. Being kind to a stranger was no big deal. It's just what he does.

Within this story lies the truth that when you make yourself vulnerable, without guile or manipulation, many people want to support you. An open, trusting view will always elicit more support than a closed and protective one.

Too many leaders I come in contact with are afraid to show vulnerability to their staffs, especially during difficult times. True, people want to follow someone who has vision and confidence. But completely confident and self-assured people who never show vulnerability can also create resistance and dependency.

Resistance, because of the human desire to question. Ann Repplier, a behavioral psychologist, has found that when adults speak with absolute certainty they often elicit in their audience a "Yeah, but . . ." response. That is, statements such as, "This is the best solution" or "We must never do that" automatically generate counter arguments. Repplier concludes that it is part of the human nature to question absolute statements.

Dependency, on the other hand, is created when I feel I have nothing to offer. If the answers are always there, the choices already made, I ultimately end up giving away my initiative, inspiration, and creativity. I become dependent on my leaders rather than offering my own thoughtful solutions. A leader who appears invulnerable, never showing anything but complete confidence and certainty, will eventually create a workforce with a somewhat warped view of reality. It is a style that has its value, especially in times of crisis. But U.S. general George Patton and British prime minister Winston Churchill were neither effective nor wanted once the war that made them prominent came to an end.

Instead, I encourage leaders to occasionally show personal vulnerability during difficult times. The statement, "I am not sure about this, but I need your help to make this work," will probably generate more support than

"I am fully confident about this solution and I know you will endorse it."

You may find that the world, even the world of work, is more benevolent than you once thought.

THINK THIRD STAGE

Beware of unintended consequences.

—Walter Peterson

In its natural food cycle, a lion in the wild eats approximately one zebra every two weeks. In a lion's lifetime, that's about 360 zebras. Note: The lions don't eat all the zebras. They manage their needs within the context of their environment. A similar balance can exist in business as well as in nature.

In describing the way a wild field grows, biologists use a model—forest ecology—that provides a powerful metaphor for today's business. Forests grow in naturally shifting stages. In the first stage, a few species of fast-growing plants will typically dominate a landscape. An example would be an unmanaged field covered with weeds of various kinds like goldenrod, some wildflowers, bushes, and different trees. The primary goal of all the plants that live in such a field is to extract the maximum amount of nutrients from the soil in order to create large quantities of seed, which they then broadcast to other areas. The goal is rapid growth and expansion, regardless of the cost. This has essentially been the entrepreneurial model of American business.

However, once the nutrients in the soil no longer meet the needs of the plants, they must move to new areas to exploit, adapt to the new conditions, or become extinct. The entrepreneurial model can work only if limitless resources exist.

In the natural field, however, there is another stage with its own compelling lesson. In this stage—stage three —the environment has much less topsoil (i.e., resources), so the strategy among species is to rely on a more complex interdependency (stage two is the transition period). There are no wasted byproducts. Each byproduct serves as a valuable resource for another. Now, instead of mass broadcasting seed to expand into other areas, there is a delicate balance of niches within one area. This helps ensure a system of self-renewal and sustainability. Interestingly, the resource limits of this stage actually stimulate more creative adaptation than is found in stage one.

I am going to talk heresy here for a minute. Why not see the world of your business as a field in which to cooperate and thrive? Don't blow away your competition all at once—even if that's possible—without being aware of the consequences of your actions. Don't be quick to level the field and claim dominance without fully understanding the implications.

An interesting case of stage three thinking is Shell Oil US. In the 1970s, Shell dominated the Gulf of Mexico in terms of production and market share to such a degree that they risked putting all of their much-needed partners out of business. Their response was to recognize that they needed a more creative, cooperative approach to managing the limited resources of the business environment. Shell set up a school to educate their vendors, partners, and competitors about what they were doing and how they were doing it. The results were stronger partnerships and ultimately a more successful and profitable Shell Oil.

During changing times, be careful that you can manage and control all you create. Think about the impact of highly competitive postures, and where you may be able to form alliances in ways that seem foreign or even radical. Consider your business environment as a field of growing, interconnected creatures, and imagine what resources will be needed not just for short-term growth but long-term sustainability. Forward-thinking organizations don't consume needed long-term resources. Instead, they proactively create strategies that promote growth with vision, recognizing the business environment as a resource to grow, not a mine to be stripped.

NAME THE DISTRACTIONS

When I say "go," try *not* to think
of an elephant. Go!

—Old Joke

Recently I was at a conference where a major captain of industry was scheduled to speak to a large lunchtime gathering. As is typical of such venues, the meal plates were cleared away and the speaker was introduced during dessert. The introduction was given by a very polished presenter, and the speaker's list of credentials was quite impressive: chairman of a major corporation, pillar of the community, friend of presidents—the list went on and on. Just as the presenter was saying, "and he holds a Harvard Law degree," one of the huge round trays, each with 40 to 50 tall champagne flutes filled with chocolate mousse, fell off the shoulder of a waiter, sending glass and mousse all over the floor. The crash was of epic proportions. You know the "room buzz" that typically follows such a crash. Today was no exception. But the introduction went on with no acknowledgment of the mishap.

A minute later, as the introduction continued a second tray—unbelievably—was dropped by a different waiter. By now, everyone was laughing, but there was still no comment about the absurdity of the situation. As the speaker got up and started his comments from the podium, a waitress dropped a third tray, right in front of him! By now the audience was nearly apoplectic. But still no response to the bizarre nature of the moment. It was a full ten minutes before the room really quieted down, and unfortunately a great deal of what was said by the speaker was missed.

I don't know for sure how an acknowledgment of the absurdity would have changed the room dynamics, but I am certain it would have helped quiet us sooner. Pretending that everything was normal, when clearly it was anything but, only served to throw fuel on the fire.

I have been in many organizations during change efforts when tough issues arose out of left field. When this happens, too many leaders err on the side of "heads down, eyes forward, take the hill," regardless of what the environment is presenting.

The lesson is clear—when distractions are present, name them! Don't pretend that everything is fine and proceed as if the status quo is intact, when it is clearly out of control. In extreme circumstances, make sure everyone knows you know by acknowledging the condition. Not doing so can create a credibility gap that is hard to close.

I had one client firm that, during a critical cultural change effort, became the target of an outside acquisition attempt. The company president decided not to talk about it publicly for fear that it might demotivate the troops. Of course, the rumors spread like wildfire, and the employees became suspicious of anything he said because they all knew there was something he wasn't telling them. Ultimately, I convinced him to come clean in appropriate ways, and once he did, morale increased, his credibility rose sharply, and productivity went up.

This doesn't mean, of course, that you dwell on life's absurdities or promiscuously spread private information. There's a fine line between acknowledging problems and creating a self-fulfilling negative prophecy. Use your best judgment. But a simple statement, reaffirming your goals while naming the distracting issue, may allow the organization to move on rather than veer off-course because of an unspoken yet unavoidable distraction.

DO THE DECENT THING

Feelings are everywhere. Be gentle.

—J. Masai

Glendon Johnson, former chairman of John Alden Insurance, is a remarkable man. Chairman of the Boy Scouts of America, Harvard Law School graduate, owner of the second largest ranch in Utah (Ted Turner's is the largest), he has a broad range of accomplishments beyond his notable business successes. Furthermore, Johnson is kind and generous, and listening to him talk about his family is a personal and intimate experience, even when there are 300 people in the room.

Johnson is also deeply committed to wellness in the workplace, and so, a number of years ago, he started a crisis and prevention center at John Alden corporate headquarters, a place that could stabilize employees in the event of a health trauma and also provide early-warning diagnostics. All this, of course, is free of charge to the employee—but quite costly to the corporation.

Recently, Johnson asked the center's nurse to go back three years and tell him what impact the program had made. He wanted to know what results the center had achieved and whether it had been worth the company's investment of capital and staff time.

The report he received was stunning. The interventions made by the center had saved the lives of five cardiac arrest victims and victims of four other critical traumas that would likely have been terminal. The center's staff also detected three early-stage cancers that would also likely have been fatal—a total of 12 lives probably saved.

What about the economic value of the center? Johnson responds with a question: "What's a life worth? I have a whole department of actuaries that price lives to the penny, and I still can't answer that question. Sometimes, the only response is to just do the decent thing." This is a man who on his initial company interview said, "If all anyone takes home from their job is a paycheck, then they take home too little."

Now consider the following statement by one lawyer to another in the midst of a dispute: "Bill, this is a whore's game. Don't play it like a virgin."

During tough times, tough decisions are frequently needed. But the clarity of how to choose and what values to act upon is not always present. The signposts are murky at best, and no clear path seems evident. During such moments, the answer is simple—do the decent thing.

Over the long haul, a leader's ability to motivate often requires a willing suspension of disbelief on the part of the employees. It is often a matter of faith based on little more than history and intuition. During these times, a reputation for decency—which is truthful, compassionate, and thoughtful consideration for others—plays an enormous role in how an organization responds.

I am reminded of a story told by Ron Woodyard, the president of Florida's Wellness Council. He was at the funeral of a friend and was deeply moved by the eulogy delivered by the man's son. The son went on and on about the impact this man had made in the community, his business, and family. Ron turned to his own 12-year-old son and said, "Russell, when I die, you have to do that for me."

His son responded, "Dad, you have to live it first."

When it comes to decency at work, what are you living? And what do you want people to be saying about you? It is not that complicated, really. Remember Glendon Johnson's advice: Do the decent thing.

THE POWER OF PRESENCE

Mr. Duffy lived just a short
distance from his body.

—James Joyce

One night, I went to see the Temptations. This was the music I grew up with. In our neighborhood, all the kids would spend every weekend dancing to Motown music. There was no Rolling Stones, Beatles, or Monkees music at our gatherings—just the Temptations, the Four Tops, Smokey, Aretha, and of course, the Supremes. All we did from early morning to the end of the day was dance, dance, dance. And not only did we dance the newest numbers coming out, like "the pony," but we also worked on our Temptation dance routines, spinning, turning, and pointing to our imaginary audiences. We danced because it took us to another place. We danced because it brought us close together. We danced because our young, growing bodies couldn't stop once the rhythm started.

So you can imagine my excitement last night when I went to see my childhood idols. And truth be told, they put on quite a show. This is a group that has for 39 years and 52 albums maintained a distinctive and memorable style. They did all the old favorites—"My Girl," "Papa was a Rolling Stone"—and they danced as they always did, clad in bright yellow outfits and matching shoes, with a 20-piece band as back-up.

Yet when I left, I felt both the joy of having seen a great performance, and that small, disquieting feeling that comes from a sense of loss. It started when they announced that only one member on stage was an original Temptation. It grew when they told us they had just returned from Las Vegas. And it grew a little more when they declared how great it was to be in New Hampshire. (Half the audience was over 60, they were all white and barely moving, for God's sake. How great could it have been?)

But mostly, they talked the way they danced. That is, their patter was stylized and smooth, but obviously had been done in just the same way hundreds of times before. When they left the stage after a show that lasted a little over an hour and the lights went on without an encore, I felt I had been watching less a pop group and more a time-honored production, like the long-running *Cats* on Broadway.

I didn't feel the passion, dynamism, or power of the group as I did when I was younger. Instead, I felt I was watching a reflection of a reflection of something I had always loved—a shadow rather than a living image.

Don't get me wrong. The Temptations were very good that night—excellent, in fact. But despite their polished style, it was hard to connect with them as an audience member. They were so smooth and so thoroughly rehearsed that there was nothing in their show that made me feel special watching them—certainly not the connection I used to feel when I was younger.

Whether it's fair to think that that youthful spirit could ever be recaptured, I don't know. But I did miss terribly the sense I used to have, the joy of feeling deeply moved, figuratively and literally, by their performance. I missed the connection.

It is very tempting to rely on old behaviors, even when they somehow disconnect us from the very people with whom we need to be in contact. During any change, we look for authenticity and presence from our leadership. And when leaders are inauthentic in their behaviors, it is seen and known. The distance that gets created can be distracting at best, disastrous at worst.

I had a consulting client who was a vice president of a major sports team. During my initial meeting with Rick (not his real name), as he talked about the organization's struggles and his lack of connection to his staff, he accepted seven phone calls in less than 40 minutes. When I interviewed members of his staff, they all talked about his lack of authenticity. Rick was always off doing something in his mind, looking for the next conversation, the next idea, rather than focusing on the here and now. He was a nice guy, but you never had a sense that when he spoke with you he was really all there—ever.

During our second conversation following my interviews with his staff, an important time, Rick accepted nine more calls, including one from a friend who was having an affair and wanted to borrow Rick's beach house. You certainly didn't get the feeling that he really cared—which of course, he didn't. He was fired a little while later for not being able to generate confidence in the organization.

It is critical that, no matter how busy you are, you take some time every day to be present—truly present—with your staff. Let's be real: If you are going through a change process, then time is not abundant. Multiple priorities, exploding phone calls, meetings, and constant interruptions are all part of the game.

You can start by placing a small stick-on dot on your watch. Every time you check the time and see the dot, take ten seconds to check in and be present. Do nothing but breathe and observe.

This attention process prepares you to do the following: Focus just 15 to 30 minutes a day where you do not allow your mind to go elsewhere—where you are fully present to the conversation—regardless of the voice that may be screaming inside your head. The Buddhists call this voice "the chattering monkey," and it needs to be periodically quieted.

If you can be present just a little bit every day with different people, then you will be given greater leeway during those many other times when you are distracted or on automatic pilot. The investment of your full and complete presence a little bit every day will give you a cushion of acceptance for those many other moments when you are unavoidably pulled away from a conversation you are still in.

THE VALUE OF A GOOD STORY

The secret is to connect the boring, important
stuff to the unimportant, interesting stuff.

—Frank Glaviano

Milton Erickson was the father of modern hypno-
therapy. He had the most amazing way of getting people
to work through their resistance and foster change. His
most frequent strategy was the effective use of stories.
Rarely did he "put anyone under" (as we might assume
hypnotherapists do), and he almost never used the "you're
getting sleepy" approach. Instead, Erickson would invite
a patient into his office and start telling him about a little
turtle with three legs or about a special car with a special
driver, and the patient would sit there wondering, "Where
is this going?"

At the end of the session, the patient would shake
Erickson's hand and leave his office, suddenly seeing the
world in a whole new way. The patient might never pick
up a cigarette again! Or might immediately start a diet
and lose 20 pounds! Erickson had used his little stories to
find a way through.

For thousands of years, humankind has told stories—
sitting around campfires or dinner tables or in pubs,

recalling the great and near-great moments of real life or myth. As humans, we are wired to respond to stories in deep, sometimes unconscious ways. We actually answer with our attention and focus, when all other efforts may fail. Watch sometime how body language changes when someone starts a joke or story. Notice the slight rise in alertness and increased presence of the listeners. People will almost always put down what they are doing and give full attention. If the teller is particularly good at storytelling, then the response is almost always deep focus.

The process of change is often a campaign to capture the hearts and minds of your people. During this struggle, a clear, visceral picture of the future that is not just known but felt can be a vital help. Stories can be a powerful tool in transcending the normal daily static that often prevents us from truly listening and understanding. They can be a way through when other methods do not work.

Many great leaders have been masterful storytellers, using narrative to create a vision that sticks hard and fast. Consider U.S. President John F. Kennedy. In response to the Soviet's early space success with the Sputnik satellite, Kennedy said to the nation, "We will send a man to the moon and return him safely." He then proceeded to paint a picture of what that would look like and why we as a nation needed to do it. He told a hell of a story, about American pride and visionary leadership. It launched the space race—a race we eventually won.

Kennedy's storytelling created an unprecedented alignment in our country that lasted through three presidents and five different congresses. The keystone of his vision was the supreme value the United States placed on human life. This focus created an attention to detail that was second to none. Kennedy's use of a visionary storytelling helped propel the country a decade later to an unimagined accomplishment that changed history forever.

So consider for a moment where you want your organization to be. What will it look like, feel like, and act like? What will the customer experience be in the new world toward which you're growing? How will departments interact and cooperate? Who will be making decisions? How will information be processed? What roles will be the same and which will be different?

I am not just talking about a laundry list of facts or figures. You must feel it—in your blood if necessary—so you can convey a sense of reality beyond sheer information. Don't worry about how you will get there. That's not initially important. It only matters that you have the vision. Ed Lindaman, NASA's first planning director, had a helpful way of viewing this. He spoke of the 250,000-mile trip to the moon as a process of very small incremental changes to the flight plan. The longest trip could be made with the smallest of course corrections. But this requires one critical condition: You must know where you're going.

Get the story of your organization's future in your head. Try to see it as clearly as your breakfast this morning. Talk to yourself in the shower or driving into work until the story is as clear. Once you've gotten it, there is only one thing left to do—tell it, tell it, tell it!

DO YOUR RESEARCH

I have every sympathy with the American
who was so horrified by what he had read about
the effects of smoking that he gave up reading.

—Henry G. Strauss

The California Institute of Technology is housed on a
beautiful and classic campus in Pasadena. Appropriately
enough for the home of the world's leading earthquake
research center, Cal Tech sits on the San Andreas fault
and is prone to frequent shifts in the earth, both small and
large.

A number of years ago, Cal Tech's board of directors
was trying to decide whether to insure their buildings for
earthquake insurance. The cost was quite steep, and all
the buildings were already built to 150 percent of the
then-existing safety code. But they wanted to be responsible and were concerned. So they brought the best minds
in earthquake research from their faculty together and
asked, "If the big one hits, which of our buildings will not
survive?" After careful analysis, the experts decided that
two of the many buildings on campus were in jeopardy.
So the Cal Tech board negotiated a deal with their insurance company to insure only those two structures.

In 1971, the San Fernando earthquake, the most destructive earthquake in state history, registering 7.1 on the Richter Scale, struck California. Hundreds of millions of dollars in damage were done all over Southern California, and Pasadena was near the epicenter. At Cal Tech, of all the buildings on campus only two were destroyed— the two predicted by their faculty, the two buildings that were insured!

At first, the insurance company didn't want to pay. They said Cal Tech had "inside information" that somehow invalidated the policy (although the company eventually made good). Clearly it was a ploy not to have to pay at settlement. But all Cal Tech really had was a scientific desire to know the facts.

The moral is clear—never underestimate the value of basic research.

One of the great joys of my job is that I get to spend a lot of time with CEOs. The benefits can be enormous, though they may not be what you might think. It's not that great minds or entrepreneurial spirits are so inspiring, although that's sometimes true. What I value is the perspective I get. CEOs tend to think that their problems, whatever they are, are the most important ones on earth and that they are the first people ever to experience them. Of course, if all these CEOs think they are the first, then probably none of them are.

I am not trying to minimize the importance of the daily business struggle. It can be a hard and competitive world. But the truth is that there's little in the world of business that hasn't already been said or done. New ground does get broken, but when it does it is often built on current learnings and practices.

The good news is that, if you are willing to look for them, there are all kinds of models that can provide inspiration and ideas outside of the small perspective of your specific problem.

During changing times, do your research. Find out who has gone before you and what they have learned. Be like the Cal Tech board—scrupulous in your desire to know and then act on that knowledge. In business history, there exist hundreds of correlations to your specific situation. Search them out, find them, become a fanatic of learning about others who have walked the path before you. Talk to colleagues, friends, and associates and do whatever it takes to get out of your enclosed view of your problem by seeking more expansive sources of information.

And don't just limit yourself to the *Wall Street Journal, Fortune,* and the business section of the bookstore. Instead look for ideas and inspiration that may come from unexpected places. I know one CEO currently going through a merger who starts every day by reading a small section of the *I Ching*—the Chinese book of changes. He told me that everything he needs to know about managing complex growth can be found within its pages.

Another client who is a software entrepreneur faithfully rereads the book *Endurance,* by Alfred Dunning, every year. It is the story of the turn-of-the-century explorer Ernest Shackleton and his abortive South Pole expedition. Early in the journey, his ship, *The Endurance,* became locked in an ice floe and was crushed. Under conditions that could only be described as inhumanly horrendous, with only the food they could catch, equipped with canvas tents, three small boats, and sheer determination, Shackleton kept his entire crew alive for almost a year and a half. They were finally rescued when Shackleton sailed over 800 miles in a 20-foot boat to seek help at a distant whaling station.

The executive told me, "I read Shackleton's story time and again to remember that anything I may be dealing with is nothing compared to his struggles. He not only showed the value of determination against all odds, he did so with a caring and concern for all his men. He brought the whole team back alive."

Part of your job during any change is to keep your mind open and yourself inspired. Get every bit of information you can from any source you can think of. Read biographies and histories, interview experts, go to art openings, attend concerts and sporting events. Never forget the value of research, in whatever realm it appears.

EMOTIONS DON'T KNOW LOGIC

Reduce intellectual and emotional noise until you arrive at the silence of yourself.

—Richard Brautigan

When my first marriage ended, my wife and I had a very civil parting. We divided up the furniture of the house using a kind of you-take-this-room-I'll-take-that approach. The big decisions were made in about ten minutes. I then suggested that I leave for the weekend so my wife could take whatever she felt was fair from the countless smaller stuff. I ended by saying, "I trust you." When I came home on Sunday night to a half-empty home, it was admittedly a bit shocking—but, all in all, I feel my ex-wife did the job with a lot of integrity.

Yet about two weeks later I found myself on the phone arguing with her over some small nonsense about who had taken what. In the heat of the argument, I heard myself screaming, "And furthermore, you took all the goddamned napkin rings!" Please note: I have never used a napkin ring, I have never liked napkin rings, I have never bought a napkin ring. This did not stop me from having a hell of a hissy-fit about napkin rings.

In looking back on this moderately embarrassing personal moment, I can reach only one conclusion—emotions don't know logic. This truth has stayed with me these many years as a grounding beacon during almost any substantial change I witness in the lives of individuals or organizations.

During the stress that accompanies change, we often hope that a cool and logical demeanor will prevail. After all, it just makes sense to sit down and discuss a problem or strategy calmly and clearly. However, in difficult times, the call of illogical emotion is a strong and powerful one. When mergers and partnerships between seemingly logical parties fail, it's usually because of the powerful emotional weight that is brought to bear. Take the well-publicized dispute between former Disney president Jeffrey Katzenberg and Disney CEO Michael Eisner. To read the newspaper accounts of their battles, replete with mutual accusations, name-calling, sarcasm, and bile, you'd think you were reading about third-graders squabbling at recess, not two of the most successful and powerful men in Hollywood. Katzenberg was once quoted as saying, "Every great story has three main elements—greed, love, and ego. One of those elements was missing from this story. And it wasn't greed or ego." That's how we humans sometimes get.

During these moments, when the full moon is up and the wolves are howling, focus your attention away from the issue and ask yourself, "Why am I getting so emotional? What's really going on?" Often the trigger has little or nothing to do with the current issue and is instead tied to other emotional fears. A banker who explodes over a small transaction problem may really be upset over larger fears of feeling trapped or helpless in a job he no longer likes. A CEO erupting over the details of who will report to whom after a proposed merger may be reliving child-hood hurts over feeling unloved and unappreciated.

In situations where your reaction defies logic—and it can happen—then logic will not help you find a solution. In the martial art of aikido, you may find yourself on a mat in a position where no amount of effort will keep you from getting hurt. But there is always a choice left to the student—to walk off the mat. In the "mat" of the orga-nization, when emotion is overruling your ability to man-age effectively, it's responsible to do the same thing.

THE IMPORTANCE OF MIDDLE MANAGEMENT

I've been promoted to middle management.
I never thought I'd sink so low.

—Tim Gould

So far in this book, I've spent a lot of time on the sub-ject of communication because I believe it is so critical. But change is about more than communication—much

more. It requires the development of trusting relationships between those who do the work and those who manage the work at the point of production.

The sad paradox is that middle management is often
disempowered during change processes, even though they
are the group that is most needed during tough times. No
CEO, no matter how articulate or charismatic, can have a
relationship with 20,000 people—these people must have
local leaders. Middle management allows senior leadership
to touch the multitudes of staff that need to be consistently engaged yet cannot be reached personally.

In at least half of my consulting engagements, the
problem of middle management is highlighted. The problem is usually a disenfranchised and demotivated work
group. I've found that two basic issues always drive the
problem—lack of communication and lack of appreciation.

First, let's briefly examine the issue of communication.
What's needed can be summed up in one word—more! As
we've seen, communication is usually underexecuted by a
factor of ten. Finding proactive ways to keep information
flowing is essential to keeping middle management
engaged. The last thing you want is for your middle to feel
embarrassed because they lack information regarding the
organization's future. It doesn't take long for embarrassment to turn to frustration and frustration to anger. Your
attempts to keep a communications link with middle management will pay off handsomely in the end with more
loyalty, satisfaction, and positive role modeling.

The second issue is appreciation. In my experience, the key issue in appreciation among middle management is one of equity—fairness. In particular, middle managers must feel that the pain caused by change is fairly and equally distributed throughout the organization. If they feel their area is viewed as a disproportionate part of the problem and thus will bear a disproportionate part of the cost of solving it, motivation will often be replaced with feelings of resentment. This gets translated down through their people and the repercussions can be huge.

As you progress through change, keep your middle mangers fully informed about the reasons for the change and the effects on their individual departments. Make sure that all questions, particularly "Why us?" questions, are answered quickly and clearly. If you want your middle managers to feel committed, then behave accordingly.

TEST YOUR ASSUMPTIONS

Listen to your listening.
Be aware of thought.
Slow down the inquiry.
Suspend assumptions and certainties.

—David Boehm

In every change initiative, there are underlying assumptions and beliefs that must be dealt with. Sometimes those assumptions are helpful, setting norms and expectations that can raise the bar for everyone. For example, the assumption that as an organization we are capable of implementing a positive change can help pull employees along in its wake. It creates a sense of belief that engenders hope and courage during tough times.

However, also remember that some assumptions can set in motion beliefs that are false or incorrect. Sadly, history is filled with these. The tragedy of the *Titanic,* for example, was caused by the false assumption that the great liner was unsinkable. Based on this belief, a series of flawed decisions was made, from equipping the ship with an inadequate supply of lifeboats to maintaining a dangerously high speed through waters in which icebergs had been spotted. Eleven hundred lives were lost as a result.

Under the pressure of change, our tendency is to move quickly to action. It is only natural. It is also natural that untested assumptions can drive behaviors—assumptions that may not be true, yet take on a life of their own. It is essential that you slow down to examine your own assumptions and the assumptions of others so that decisions are made based on reality and not fiction.

In the early days of the turnaround of Sears & Roebuck, the once-troubled retail giant, Sears employees were under the impression that 45 cents out of every dollar paid for Sears merchandise went into the company coffers as profit. This false belief created enormous tension between line employees and management. When this assumption was discovered, the employees were surprised to learn that the figure was actually around two cents. Replacing a false assumption with the facts made reality-based communication and planning possible and the turnaround was able to proceed successfully.

Recently, I worked with the executive teams from two merging companies. I asked the team members to individually write down what they believed were the responsibilities of each team member. They listed these work roles under three categories: "mine," "yours," and "ours." The CEO had never thought to ask the team members to test their assumptions about these responsibilities because essentially it was clear to him. The results were eye-opening. For instance, two different people thought they were in charge of a major research initiative, when, in fact, in the eyes of the CEO, neither of them was! By working through these assumptions and verifying the real facts, we avoided enormous potential problems down the road.

The lesson is clear: Test your assumptions, test your assumptions, test your assumptions! If you don't, you open yourself up to a world of potential pain.

TWO KINDS OF MOTIVATION

I'm not into working out.
My philosophy: No pain, no pain.

—Carol Leifer

Sunrise Assisted Living is a very successful health care organization with a strong mission. A $300 million company, it is growing at an average rate of 40 percent a year. Sunrise is targeted to double within the next two years, which is strong in anyone's book.

What makes Sunrise so special is not its growth, though it is spectacular in a business that has taken a real beating, but its strict adherence and fanatical pride to its core assumption. It is written on the business card of every employee and reads: "Belief in the sacred value of human life." Sunrise takes its mission very seriously.

Operating predominately in the United States, where the prevailing culture is essentially one that devalues senior adults, Sunrise sees its role as an advocate for "elders" rather than as processing "the elderly." When you speak with Sunrise's Executive Vice President of Operations Tiffany Tommaso, it is clear that the company takes pride in swimming up the cultural stream of pessimism. Instead of providing typical care, Sunrise prefers to be agents for elder dignity.

Founder and CEO Paul Klaassen believes so much in Sunrise's values of respect and joy in service that he actually talks about something called the second paycheck. It works like this.

The second paycheck is the payment one receives above and beyond the compensation of money. It is a payment in kind that comes from knowing you are doing something of worth and making a difference. Klaassen believes every employee in every facility should feel like he or she is getting a second form of compensation, that is, something of deep value that, in addition to money, is a form of payment.

At best, in most organizations, this value-added compensation is unspoken. Occasionally, some companies give it lip service. Sunrise really believes in the concept of the second paycheck and actively hires and promotes to this principle. Typically, employees are first selected and then consistently reminded of this cultural bias.

But it is more than that. Besides serving the critical function of reinforcing Sunrise's strong and value-based culture, the second paycheck also allows employees to express their own altruistic values on a continuing basis.

An important lesson can be learned from Sunrise. Most organizations have the potential to create a second paycheck; somewhere, somehow, profit or nonprofit, an inherent second paycheck usually exists. It can be about service or customer concerns, innovation or cutting-edge values, or improving the community. The focus can be on anything that you as an organization find essential and employees intrinsically value.

In his landmark work on motivation, Abraham Maslow postulates that at the top of every human's list is the desire to find meaning. The second paycheck is a living, breathing example of a value-based approach reflecting Maslow's concept. And because most people want to see, grasp, and feel their impact, that is, to make a difference, creating second-paycheck thinking in your organization and reinforcing it on a consistent basis can have a powerful influence.

I see many leaders during change efforts talking about the benefits to the company or their departments, but rarely the benefits to the individuals they're addressing. It's as if they assume that, because something is a benefit to them, it will be a benefit to their people, or, conversely, that because something is not a benefit to them, it will not be a benefit to someone else.

Mereyem LeSaget, France's leading change consultant, is a delightful friend and colleague of mine. Her views of motivation are fascinating and important.

LeSaget believes that all motivation can be fit into one of two types—*transactional* and *intrinsic*. Transactional motivations are short-term and based on immediate needs. They include such things as stock options, money, promotional opportunities, and job security. Intrinsic motivations are long-term and are more related to the emotional growth of the individual.

LeSaget places these intrinsic motivations in the following ascending order. The first is meeting the inherent curiosity needs of the employee; that is, their basic aspiration to learn and explore. The second is their desire to grow; that is, to develop and improve as a professional. The third is the need to find a greater sense of meaning and purpose in work.

LeSaget believes that management can effectively satisfy all forms of transactional motivations, if it so desires, as well as the first two intrinsic motivations. Money, learning, and growth are all prerogatives of leadership to bestow. However, meaning is something that can only be provided by the individual.

The implications of these insights for organizations going through change are critical. First, realize that providing monetary incentives only may not be sufficient for your employees' long-term growth. Working with a group of senior money managers at an international bank recently, we got into a discussion of "hitting the wall." It was clear that everyone in the group had calculated what they called their "f**k-you number"—the amount of savings they'd need to bail from their jobs and do something else with their lives. One trader said, "I think about that amount every single day!" Every bonus, every monetary incentive seemed to motivate them for a couple of weeks, and then they were back to focusing on their number— until the next bonus, six months or a year later.

It's not that money isn't important. But the more you have of it, the less it will motivate you. Yet, paradoxically, the more you have of it, the more you assume that it is all about the money. It is not.

Another crucial implication is that it's important to provide your staff not just with transactional incentives but with the first two intrinsic motivations as well. When you want long-term commitment, find ways to reward people with growth and learning. Focus on more than money. Money rarely provides stability or loyalty—regardless of what you may think.

A case in point is this absurd downsizing strategy that seems to be sweeping corporate America. When a company needs to reduce its head count, they will typically send out voluntary "retirement packages" to many of their employees. If the employee responds with a "yes," they will give him or her a decent settlement. But if the employee refuses the offer and is subsequently laid off, then the settlement package is significantly smaller. This puts employees in a painful game of high-stakes poker. If they leave on their own, it can be very difficult but rarely fatal; but if the employees guess wrong and stay, they are in for a world of hurt.

The cruel kicker is this: If the employee decides to leave and accept the company's offer (and imagine the difficulty of that decision), the company isn't obligated to honor it! An employee can go through the entire emotional struggle of readying himself or herself for the exit, only to be pulled back into the organization to help with the transition. Who is the organization kidding? And we as a society wonder why there is no more company loyalty!

As a change leader, you must balance the motivations you provide. Don't just offer money, but generate growth and learning opportunities as well. But realize that the second key—meaning from one's job—does not and cannot come from the organization. It can only come from within.

FOUR INGREDIENTS OF CHANGE

Whatever you can do, or dream you can, begin it. Boldness has genius, power, and magic in it.

—Goethe

There are four prerequisites to effective change. If any one is missing from the puzzle, the chances of success are seriously reduced. The four ingredients are: (1) a clear, shared vision; (2) the internal capacity for change; (3) an external pressure for change; and (4) actionable first steps. Let's take them one at a time.

The first requirement is a clearly articulated and compelling vision. You first have to convince your people the problem is worth fixing, which requires the creation and communication of a picture that the organization really understands and accepts. The simpler the better. For instance, Jack Welsh of General Electric once said, "There are three things I need to run any company and grow shareholder value: customer satisfaction, employee satisfaction, and cash." In this simple, direct formula, there is no confusion over what he needs or where he wants to go.

This vision must be shared and owned by those responsible for carrying it out. It also needs to speak to their dreams and hopes, to have fire and meaning, and to reflect a higher value. Consider President Franklin D. Roosevelt. When Roosevelt was elected in 1932, the United States had the 14th largest army in the world. And yet within a few years, a few brave men—led by Roosevelt—decided to buck the tide of isolationism and take on Hitler's war machine, the greatest military force of its time. The nation followed Roosevelt to victory. That was a vision of courage, decisiveness, and focus.

If you do not have a clearly shared vision—one that people are excited about and believe in—then the result will usually be a fast start that fizzles out.

The second essential building block is the internal capacity to change. It's unfair and anxiety-producing when individuals are asked to adjust without the necessary support and training. This includes not just technical skills but values and attitudes as well. Change is like estate planning—most people never want to do it or even think about it; but unlike estate planning, you hope you don't have to die to get the benefits. Your goal is to get your organization trained for change without the corporate body going to room temperature. Otherwise, it's like having 500 people on the highway learning to drive by doing.

You'll know you've won the hearts and minds of your people when they exhibit values essential to the effort. Frank Glaviano is a senior manager with Shell Oil whose responsibilities include safety. Frank knows that a slip in safety protocol can mean death to one of his people. He gets most excited when he goes to an employee's house and sees them behaving in their homes with the same high safety standards that Frank mandates on an oil rig.

The third ingredient is an external pressure to change. It is essential that your people know how high the pressure is for change in today's hypercompetitive environment. If they don't, you are in big trouble. In a world where so many people spend their time at work putting out fires, what has priority and what does not is a reflection of how much external pressure is being brought to bear. When you ask people to undertake a major change effort, make sure that there is a real market-driven reason for the effort. Otherwise you run the risk of being seen as the company Chicken Little. There are only so many times you voice the same warnings about the need for change without being seen as an alarmist and a worrywart.

The last essential ingredient is actionable first steps— consistent and sustainable actions that move the organization toward the vision. But don't confuse movement for action. Anyone who has participated in the so-called quality movement over the past ten years has noted the difference between these two. Don't get me wrong—I am all for quality, and Dr. Edwards Deming and the other quality gurus have played a huge positive role in American business. But the quality movement has undeniably created a pattern of movement without action. How many times have you heard people describe quality efforts with phrases like, "We met, and met, and met, and met, and nothing happened"? Too many quality meetings are little more than Roach Motels for good ideas—they go in, but they don't come out. The key is to make sure you plan change actions that are deliberate, sustainable, and directly related to the vision. The key word is *consistency:* Make the actions consistent, make the rewards consistent, and manage the process in a consistent manner.

If not, you will end up making many false starts and half-hearted attempts. Start with a visible, practicable action that you know will be successful and build from there. Success builds on success. Remember the words of Mother Teresa: "We don't do great things. We do simple things in a great way."

Finally, be clear about what's good enough and what isn't. The 80/20 principle—we can make real progress with 80 percent accuracy—is an effective way to create movement most of the time. But there are circumstances in which 80 percent is just not good enough. Even 90 percent success is not acceptable, for instance, in a hospital delivery room. Be honest about what makes for real success. Don't overinflate the need for perfection, but be clear—very clear—about it when you do.

That is how you create effective action.

DON'T EAT YOUR SEED CORN

The time when you most need to relax is
when you don't have the time to relax.

—Unknown

In the rush of change a lot can get lost. The secret is
to be able to stay balanced in the middle of the confusion.
When surrounded by chaos, it can be very difficult to
make effective choices. Here's a case in point.

It was the kind of day that only Chicago's O'Hare Airport can provide. It was 4:00 on Friday afternoon, the
start of the Memorial Day weekend. For two hours, the
airport had been closed because of thunderstorms. It was
pandemonium, with more angry people in one place than
I'd ever seen; lines on top of lines; people screaming, ranting, crying. But, at least, after a long week on the road, I
was going home. I wanted it so badly I could taste it.

First thing I did was go and check the board for my
flight—Manchester, New Hampshire—United Airlines.
And there, in big, red letters, was the word dreaded by
every veteran flyer . . . *canceled*. Not *delayed*. Not *rescheduled*. But the C word—canceled!

I have learned not to panic. After three seconds of
deep breathing, I called my travel agent. My normal contact was not there; I heard a new voice. I started to ask

questions: "When is the next flight out? There is none? They're all booked for the next two days? Aren't there any options at all?" But there was a glimmer of hope: I was told I could get a flight to Boston at 8:00 that night, or—wait, it looked as if there was an American Airlines flight to Manchester at 5:15! If I could get a Rule 120/20 stamp on my ticket, I might just make it. (Rule 120/20 is a little-known procedure whereby, in emergencies, airlines will honor other airlines' tickets, no questions asked. In this case, it was to be my lifeline.)

With home as my carrot, I moved into attack mode, all systems go. I bullied my way to the front of a two-hour line, and, screaming, insisted that I get a Rule 120/20 stamp on my ticket so I could get home on the 5:15. My pushiness paid off. I was stamped and racing for a gate at the far end of a terminal two terminals away—apparently the official mileage the U.S. Olympic Marathon Team uses when they train.

At 5:05, I pulled up at the gate—wheezing, sweating, panting, but relieved. All I could think was "I'm going home!" As I rushed to the desk, I boomed, "Any seats?" Yes!

"Great! Here, I've been cleared—Rule 120/20," I said, flashing my ticket.

"You may go right on."

So I boarded, a conquering hero—feeling like Hannibal but looking more like Willie Loman. I settled in to my seat and began to relax. The guy next to me seemed a bit chatty, and we started up a conversation.

"Going home?" he asks.

"Oh, yes" I say with relish. "Can't wait."

"Where do you live?"

"Peterborough."

"Never heard of that town? Where is it?"

"Between Manchester and Keene," I say.

"Keene? Never heard of that either."

"You know. Keene, New Hampshire."

"New Hampshire? This plane is going to Manchester, England!"

"STOP THE PLANE!" I fled in a panic two minutes before the door was closed. I can still hear the laughter and applause from my fellow travelers. I'd like to think that today I am a wiser and humbler man.

Striving to manage change in a world driven by excess sometimes feels like attempting to recapture an elusive dream after awakening. We struggle to remember the threads, but putting the whole dream together once the real world has intruded is nearly impossible. When the daily chaos of life intrudes on our ability to effectively manage our work, our work can begin to feel like a dream.

During change efforts, leaders often feel caught in this frenzy, driven by forces over which they have little control—running from one meeting to another, leaping from e-mails to faxes to phone conferences, with demands and stress continually piling up. Everything seems equally urgent. Throw into this already confused and volatile mix the inevitable out-of-town trip of two to four days and our ability to respond effectively starts to disappear.

It's not surprising that many of us feel our lives are out of balance. Organizationally, they often are, especially during change efforts. The cruel paradox is that, at the very times we need to be most creative, we find ourselves retreating, running for cover, and feeling less and less confident.

A story is told about the student and devotee of a mystic guru who went to visit her for the first time in her native India. He reached the guru on her deathbed. As he approached, he said, "Mother, I am lost. All I see around me is poverty. I want to give away my shoes, my clothes, my money, my airplane ticket, everything I own. But if I do that, I don't know how I will get home. Tell me, what should I do?"

The guru leaned forward, took his hand, and whispered, "Spend only your interest—never your capital!"

Leaders often miss this truth in times of crisis. They spend their personal capital—emotional, physical, and psychological—without nurturing themselves in the process. With their inner resources depleted, all they experience is fatigue and fear. Among the Navaho, this state is called "eating your seed corn." I call it an addiction to frenzy.

We can't control the pace of change and its demands. But we can manage the daily care taking of our spirit and of the health and personal relationships that are the foundation of all our success.

If you can't take care of yourself, you can't take care of your business. Spend time rejuvenating your batteries, and do it every day. Exercise, walk, read, listen to music, play with your kids—it doesn't matter what you do so long as it is consistent and it replenishes you.

Are you eating your seed corn—spending your spiritual capital? Depleting yourself may work in the short term, but you will sacrifice the ability to make wise decisions in critical moments.

RE-MEMBER YOUR DREAM

One's philosophy is not best expressed in words. It is expressed in the choices that we make, and those choices are ultimately our responsibility.

—Eleanor Roosevelt

"Today like every other day we wake up frightened and alone. Do not go to the library to read a book. Instead, take down a musical instrument. Let the beauty of what you love, be what you do. There are a thousand ways to kneel and kiss the ground."

These words by the 12th century Sufi poet Jellaludin Rumi reflect the dilemma we fall into when we fail to follow our heart's dream. How many times at work have you felt, if not frightened, either alone, isolated, misunderstood, taken advantage of, unsure, or burnt out? And the list goes on.

Under the pressures of change, we can leave our values, our beliefs, our core dreams in the dust. They fall away because of fear—fear of failure, fear of looking bad, fear of what will happen if we just present to the world who we really are. Yet those core dreams don't just disappear. They fester in us and rankle, stewing away as a sad reminder of what might have been. That's the heaviest price we pay.

I believe we all have the capacity to call up those dreams that once fueled our passions. But when we forget our fire, it creates a barren numbness that eventually leads us to join life's walking dead. You can see them every day, trudging into work, passionless and depressed, ready to face the day with a *carpe mortem* attitude.

Many of us are playing a game at work—a productive, sometimes lucrative game, but a game nonetheless. We have lost the capacity to ask, "What do I really want, and how can I seek it in my place of work?"

Forget the "yes, buts" that bubble out of us like a litany of "begats" out of the Bible: "My company can't . . . ," which begat "My boss won't . . . ," which begat "My job isn't . . . ," which begat "My employees never . . . ," and so on.

The critical need is to *re-member* (literally, to rejoin) those dreams that are calling from the most authentic parts of your working soul. If you do, you'll discover what you already know.

Every summer for the past 18 years, my closest friend Rod and I have traveled to northern Canada on a reflective work retreat that puts us back in touch with our authentic selves. For half of those years, the pattern was the same. I'd get in the car and Rod would ask, "So, how are you doing?" And I would immediately begin painting a false picture of the truth: "Great. Fabulous. Couldn't be better. Life is sweet."

Yeah, right. Life was sweet in a marriage that shouldn't have been. Life was great during a painful divorce. Life was terrific when I was struggling with a tough client who was making me (physically and psychologically) sick. I was so invested in looking good that I was running a con—on my friend and on myself.

Yet my authentic self saw through the con. And because of my friendship with Rod, after about two hours in the car, honesty would replace self-delusion. Some of the most important discussions of life I've ever had occurred on those 14-hour journeys north.

Those talks became for me a personal touchstone— the yearly place where I confronted the truth of who I was and the choices I was making. Our annual car ride became the place where honesty and integrity rose above patterns of denial.

Most important, even when my conscious mind didn't know what was wrong, my authentic self never forgot my life's dream. It knew something was wrong even when I didn't.

The gift of the authentic self is that it is relentless and merciless in helping us to remember our life's dream. We may not recognize the message (because we are steeped in lethargy or anger or depression), and we may not like the messenger (our boss, our colleagues, the corporate VP of human resources), but our authentic self wants us to receive it.

The good news is that no special requirements are necessary to learn to listen; with practice, you don't even need a trip to Canada. Sometimes the trick can be learned in just 15 minutes a day. The key is to take the time to listen.

And wherever you start on this journey is perfect for where you need to be. You may be dissatisfied. That in itself is good news. Never curse the rungs of the ladder that got you to where you are. Instead, choose to welcome this dissatisfaction as the gift it is—a message from the authentic self saying, "It's time. Wake up!" Among traditional societies, this voice is called "the wisdom voice" or "the voice of divine discontent." It is your deepest resource.

Be thankful for these feelings. Rejoice in your misery. It means you are not yet fully dead.

TWO KEYS

I use the Playtex bra as a source of inspiration.
You know their motto? "Lift and support."

—Unknown

A plan is not just about creating an idea. It is about execution—pure and simple. Many great, visionary plans fail not because the idea wasn't sound, but because people weren't able to translate the idea into sustainable change. Obviously, a great number of variables can come into play with any change transition. A cogent process can turn to dust at a moment's notice. But, and this is a big but, I have found two variables over the years that equate to sustainable change more than any other.

How important are they? Let me answer it this way. Jerry Nunally, vice president for Institutional Planning at the California Institute of Technology (*U.S. News & World Report*'s number-one U.S. university in 1999), told me the following story. His boss, the president, was querying him, after Jerry asked for money to beef up the fundraising department. The president asked, "If I give you the resources you want, can you guarantee it [an increase] will happen?" Jerry very smartly answered, "No, but I can guarantee if you don't give me the needed resources, it won't happen."

These two areas do not guarantee successful implementation. A lot needs to be put into place for achievement to occur. But without them, I can guarantee you will not be successful.

The two variables needed are (1) a force of will on the part of senior leadership and (2) consistency in that will reflected in action and behavior.

Without reservation, I feel "the force of will and consistency" are the most essential and critical elements for success. Let's face it: Every change, transition, or implementation is going to meet resistance—every one, no matter what. When it hits the fan, and they all do at some point, what is required is a tough-eyed stance from leadership that says, "Whatever it takes, we are not turning back."

I was once called in to work with one company where the franchise owners and partners, unhappy with a reorganization report from a Big Five consulting firm, burned the report outside the president's office. Please note: They did not just argue or complain. They poured lighter fluid on a leather-bound tome and set it on fire when the president was inside in a meeting with a local congressman. Irrational behavior, when survival is at stake, is often the par for the course.

In subsequent conversations with the president and his team, it soon became obvious that they had been giving mixed messages to their partners and franchise owners about their resolve and focus. In our private meetings, the president eventually had to confront his inclination to avoid conflict and his subsequent tendency to appease.

I asked him a question that Sol Linsky, the great community activist, always asked his clients. He'd say, "Do you want to change?" When they said "yes" (often too quickly), he'd ask again, "Do you *really* want to change?" When they again said "yes" he'd ask one more time, "Do you *really* want to change?" The point was made. There is no room for half-hearted effort. Change takes courage. And courage is purely a matter of character and resolve.

The lesson is clear. Make sure you are determined in your belief that the change needs to happen. This does not mean that you cannot change course in the way you implement—that goes without saying. But the goal must be clear and resolute.

With the above president and his senior team, we focused on where the lack of resolve sent mixed messages to the organization. His top leaders, sensing a lack of courage on the part of the president, started covering their positions with subtle but eroding equivocations. They became inconsistent in their messages and the behaviors that followed. This fostered an environment of half-hearted commitment, which led to the troops sensing weakness instead of resolve. The dominos fell into place with the burning of the report. But the president, by being unclear in his commitment to the final destination, had earlier lit the match.

In my work with the senior team, it became all about courage, character, and commitment. In spite of the organizational anxiety, tensions died down once the message was consistently and resolutely promoted. Saboteurs, in whatever form they promote themselves, will not act if they feel they do not have a chance for success. One of the best forms of reducing this type of resistance is through clarity of position. The message states, "We are doing this. No matter what. It won't be easy. But we are committed to our course of action and we will not be swayed."

The bottom line is that resolve promotes safety. Anything less, particularly if the leader is known for avoiding conflict, can send a message that promotes instability and fear. Remember that commitment is a series of moment-to-moment choices. And lack of commitment can often be as subtle as a series of moment-to-moment abstentions.

KEEP TO THE SHORT LIST

*The sign of true intelligence is to take a
complex problem and make it simple.*

—Ed Dewees

Last year I was in Peru when I started to get chest pains. As I was standing on a street corner in Lima clutching my chest, I suddenly recognized an important thing. I realized I had a "short list" and a "long list." The important list was the short one. Life does not get complex during chest pains. You do not need a lot of words to explain what matters. It becomes things like "I love my wife" or "Please God. Don't let me die." It is simple and rarely elegant. You just get it, whatever *it* is. The long list was everything else. Money, taxes, clients, headaches, plane schedules, etc. What was so stunning was how short the short list got and how long the long list got in a matter of seconds. Today, healthy and well, I am trying to focus on a simple action—more time on the short list and less on the long one. I am not always successful, but the intention has been helpful and surprisingly effective.

Anyone who has once gone through a life-threatening illness will tell you the same thing. When you are on your deathbed, the small details of life rarely matter. In fact, they never matter. What makes the experience so profound is when individuals can remember to focus on their short list after they are well—in the heat of daily living. That is when you know you are on the right course.

This larger-than-life lesson also has specific application to the world of business. The metaphor, in any transition, should always be, "Focus on the short list." Plain and simple, it can save you a lot of trouble and wasted energy.

Sometimes I am simply amazed about how focus can be lost to the long list when anxiety and fear take hold. You have to practice to keep the important things important.

The following is an example from a client. During a $120 million implementation project, the manager in charge was being asked almost daily for budget and speed reports. "Faster, better, cheaper" became the watchwords that drove the process. Sadly, all he heard was the word *cheaper* and he responded by spending a significant portion of his time worried about how to reduce the surplus. This led him, after much consideration, to cut back on sodas for team members and replacing the free cookies with pretzels because they were cheaper.

First, it was amazing to me that he would deny a team of 28 people, many of whom were working 12 to 16 hours a day, seven days a week, cookies to cut costs. Now truthfully, I am not a big cookie fan. But they were a hit with the team, and their loss was grumbled about for weeks. The bigger shock was that on a $120 million project of this scope and size, the focus was literally on pennies. Focusing on cheaper when what was really needed was speed seemed completely fruitless. The cost saved was insignificant to the bottom line.

So why does this happen? Let's face it. In any rational-thinking person's book, cookies should make the long list. But this is a true story, from a multinational corporation. And if you think about it, it probably occurs more than you would like to admit. It may happen all too frequently in your place of work.

At the root of this struggle sits the fear of loss of control. When we are in a difficult place, our tendency will be to try to control whatever we can, because control gives us the sense of safety. The problem is, sometimes that sense is little more than an illusion. And rarely, if ever, can we "control" the short-list issues. We can manage for them, we can promote them, we can foster them, and we can even champion them, but control them? Doubtful.

This leads for those in fear to then focus on what can be controlled. And that is usually all about the long list. Pretzels instead of cookies are a long-list item. In any given day, there are hundreds of potential additions to the list.

Your goal, simply, is to identify first what is on the short list. In your process of identification I am going to make a strong recommendation. I recommend you understand not just your organizational short list but your personal one as well.

It's important to understand this list because where we are unclear in our thinking is where we tend to be unresolved. And where we are unresolved is where we are often driven by fear. And when we are driven by fear, we often move to control and spending way too much time on the long list.

It all stems from a lack of clarity that can start with your personal lists. If you hem and haw about your key priorities, it is an indication that says, "Watch out. You are in dangerous territory."

THE PLANNING CYCLE

Plan ahead.
Noah built the ark before it started raining.

—Unknown

Years ago, during a planning meeting with a client I found myself frustrated with the roles different people were taking at the table. One manager kept finding fault in everything that was presented. He was a constant barrage of criticism. One kept going off track, and diverging into "blue skying," especially when time was running short. A third manager kept pushing for premature resolution and action every time a new idea was brought forward. He was literally pacing around the table like a caged animal. It was a challenge to keep them all on the same page and moving in the same direction. To say it was a less than successful meeting would be a massive understatement.

Leaving that day, I knew if I could help it, I never wanted to run another frustrating session like that one. I needed to be better prepared with a framework that could both help manage the process while promoting rather than diminishing the participants' strengths. They were all incredibly gifted, bright, and motivated individuals, so my goal was to enable their talents rather than suppress them. Driving my agenda regardless was not going to work. I needed help of a different type.

It was at this time I stumbled across the work of Roger Von Oeck. A brilliant creativity specialist, Von Oeck had developed a theory of creative problem solving that had direct application to the meetings I was running. His theories, which I've adapted to a planning model, have significantly helped move groups forward in a way that also promotes the skills of all involved.

The thinking is that in any planning process there are four distinct and different skill sets that need to be played. These four roles are essential to almost any successful venture. They can be used for either a single meeting or for a longer, more involved implementation process. They can reflect the attributes of different team members or they can be representative of types of thinking used by one person. The theory works equally well in either scenario.

The key is to remember this: What will optimize the potential for results is not just what is said, but also when it is said.

The right skills, questions, and behaviors need to be elicited—but in their proper sequence. This is because the right comment at the wrong time can be as deadly as the wrong comment—*period!*

In developmental order, here's the thinking: In the planning process, there are four types of primary actions and behaviors.

The first is the process of looking at all of the possibilities. It is asking the question "What if . . . ?" The skill required is of examining all of the possibilities and keeping your options open. It is one of divergent thinking. An example might be "What if peanut butter came in slices?"

The second process crafts the ideas in a usable form. It takes the rough concept, pulled from imagination and creative thought, and like a sculptor molds the idea into a usable form. The thinking process is one of convergence. It gives shape to the distilled but still amorphous image. It might sound like, "Great idea! Let's package it like presliced cheese and call it "Nut Buddies."

The third process brings in judgment—looking for potential problems and glaring weakness. It refines through hard questions and tough examination. The role of the skeptic is called for to make sure wasted effort, let alone time and money, are not spent chasing a pipe dream. The goal is to find any fatal flaws that could potentially make the project fail. The questions are very different. Usually, they challenge with a lot of "Yes, but" statements. Comments like, "Have you thought about *this* issue?" Or "It won't work because" are typical examples. Uncovering the potential problems helps create an idea with strength and resilience.

The fourth and final process brings in activity. The voice is typically one of action. The goal is to take whatever next steps are needed to put the concept out into the world. Sometimes it's marketing, sometimes it's research, and sometimes it's selling. But it almost always is about moving away from discussion toward motion. It might sound like "Let's contract a food engineer to see if we can actually make peanut butter by the slice and a market research firm to see if kids will eat the stuff."

These four types of thinking are essential to make any change plan a reality. Each specific role plays an enormously valuable part in effective meeting management. But as mentioned earlier, it is not just what has to be done but the *proper sequencing* of this thinking. Any valuable contribution, when taken out of context, will derail and frustrate even the best of intentions.

For instance, we have all been part of a meeting where the constant pushing for action under the pressure for "results" will force a premature solution that may not hold water. Or where a skeptic will frustrate creative thought, dampen enthusiasm, and stifle out-of-the-box thinking during the early stages of discussion. On the other hand, creative brainstorming brought in when the process has moved forward to action only serves to derail whatever movement has occurred by returning the group to zero.

The key to planning change is to use a strategy of sequenced engagement; that is, involve the skills of the right people at the right time. Remember first and foremost we all want to be heard and make a contribution. Each team member can find his or her place if encouraged to contribute individual talents at the right time. Don't make the mistake of having the right components on a team but not managing the dynamics in a way that maximizes individual contribution when it is most needed.

In your next meeting, watch for the "what" and the "when" of the work. The outcomes may surprise you.

THE F-TROOP FACTOR

There are four types of soldiers in the British
army. Smart and lazy, smart and hardworking,
stupid and lazy or stupid and hardworking.
You can work with or manage any combination
but one. Stupid and hardworking!

—Field Marshall Bernard Montgomery

All this talk about change is well and good. But what
if you have a flawed, depressed organization and you are
trying to turn it around? What do you do then?

I have a client, Peter, who is a new president at an
engineering company. He was aghast at what he found
once he really started to dig in to his job. He refers to his
daily battle for change as combating the "F-Troop" factor. Remember the TV sitcom "F-Troop"? A bunch of
well-intentioned but misguided soldiers who were the
very definition of incompetence and poor judgment. I
once heard him mutter, in reference to some typical
bureaucratic stupidity, "We're the cream of the crap." It
is not an easy place to be.

In such a situation, what is your option? In my experience, turning around a suboptimizing organization
requires the effective and judicious use of leadership
power. I am not talking about power that comes from

position. "Because I said so" will only get you so far. Threats and intimidation tactics are generally not the best course of action. Remember that power has to be earned. Of course, there are exceptions to every rule, but fear is rarely a good long-term motivation when the "F-Troop" factor is present.

Browbeating will typically generate resistance, which will then go underground and subvert in insidious ways. Instead, consider power driven through relationships. Ultimately you will be more effective. But how?

Study after study have shown that power and its ability to persuade is typically generated by one of three things— expertise, dependency, or obligation.

Expertise is the most typical form. It stems from an employee's belief that you, as the leader, have essential knowledge. Peter had one major factor working for him. He was legendary in his field for his skill base. As president of another company, he had made a large fortune based on his negotiating skills. Coming into his new company, he was perceived as having instant credibility.

One immediate action he took was to flex his expertise muscles. He began by holding a series of monthly cocktail meetings that were open to all employees. During these meetings he reviewed the company's status and answered any and all questions from the floor. His knowledge base of the industry and his vision of the future provided instant credibility. He created an opportunity to shine. He knew it and played it politically as well as for the communication value. It gave him power among the masses.

The second way to garner power is through a sense of dependence employees may feel toward you as a leader. A perception of reliance means that the employee feels his or her personal success is tied to your success. That is, I will follow you because it is good for me. Peter's very presence as an industry success story, in a publicly owned company, provided him with power through faith. That faith was with all those employees whose retirement funds were tied to the stock price. They knew, if they were going to retire in style, that he was their best shot to date. Peter was not shy about consistently referring to this critical point of view. He mentioned in almost every initial employee meeting that his goal was to drive up the stock price so everyone could retire early. This statement made him a lot of friends quickly.

Obligation is the third way to garner power through relationship. It is based on the use of personal favor. The thinking is quite simple. When I do something for you, for example, provide assistance, you are then obligated to me in some way. When the favors build, or the favor is a big one, my power becomes one of obligation. The sense of indebtedness you feel gives me influence.

After his first three months on the job, Peter granted a series of small but significant requests to his key subordinates. A lateral job transfer, extended leave to care for a sick parent, and support on a key project were all actions he not only took, but looked for. Please don't misinterpret his intentions. Peter is not manipulative. He took these actions because they were the right things to do. He would have done them regardless of where he was in the organization. That is who he is. But, and this is a big but, he tried to find ways to support his staff, knowing their sense of obligation would also help him create a power base.

Power was not the intention behind his actions—but he used obligation effectively to his advantage. Turning around a difficult situation was his key charge. Any port in a storm was what was needed. He would rely on whatever he could.

Finally, aside from favors, obligation is built in one more important and essential way—when you make someone else's priorities your priorities. If you take something important to an employee, peer, or boss and put it at the top of your in-box, it creates a sense of loyalty and appreciation hard to match any other way in today's busy and turbulent world. If you can find ways of supporting the efforts of others not directly related to your work bucket, the obligation engendered is real and deep.

When you have an F-Troop organization, try using informal power as a key turn-around strategy. It may be the difference between your success and bankruptcy.

CAN PEOPLE REALLY CHANGE?

I yam what I yam and that's all that I yam.

—Popeye the Sailor

Looking back on my career, if there was one area where I had the least amount of success it would be in the area of personality turnaround. Typically, I would be called in to help coach an employee in need of "career rescue." This employee usually was on the brink, and I was seen as a last-ditch, but hope-filled effort at helping. Almost always the intention was a kind one—helping an employee in crisis. But sadly, and quite predictably, my track record of success was at best 50 percent. These experiences have taught me a tough lesson and with it a hard conclusion. Being an optimist and psychologist made it very difficult to accept. But, it is this: Simply put, people don't change that much.

Don't get me wrong. I have seen my share of behavioral turnarounds that were nothing short of miraculous. And I deeply value the loyalty that drives a supportive effort. But by and large, as a general rule, in my experience, do people really change in work environments? Not really.

A more fundamental question is, can they? That is, do I believe people have the capacity for substantial change? Of course. But, I've seen too many people, in need of their job and threatened with termination, fail to make any type of real change. When all reason would dictate a behavioral shift to the contrary, they were unable to fundamentally transform. Time and again, provided with coaching, specific action plans, support systems, and a real reason to change, clients continued to return to patterns that would in all likelihood cause a loss of their jobs. Sometimes it was mind-boggling. It couldn't have just been my lack of effectiveness. Something else was going on.

I never really understood the challenge of behavioral change until recently. It was precipitated by a short conversation with a stranger at a conference. She had heard me speak about my lifestyle leading up to open-heart surgery and engaged me in the following conversation.

"Let me understand. You saw your father die of a heart attack in front of you when you were 16 and he was 48, correct?"

"Yes"

"And you knew you had family history and high cholesterol, correct?"

"Yes, again."

"And yet you still continued to have bad eating habits and lived an unhealthy lifestyle, yes?"

"Guilty as charged."

"I only have one question. Why?"

That is a damned good question, and I have been struggling to understand the answer ever since. After all, I am in the change business, and one would think that when confronted with a behavioral change that could mean my life, I would be rather aggressive in taking action. It's not very complicated. Heart disease is the one medical condition science can predict with almost 100 percent accuracy. It is also the one condition medicine can almost always prevent (with lifestyle change). But confronted with these hard facts predicting an early death, I still was a poster boy for bad eating habits.

Behavioral change is a very complex issue. A typical combination of stubbornness, avoidance of pain, illusion, and short-term thinking can prevent even the best of us from really making progress. Mix in a little denial and it's easy to see how many behavioral change efforts go astray.

So, what does this imply? Time and again I have heard the following prophetic and compelling advice from leaders throughout my career. It is simple and profound and it can have a major impact on how you manage. Behavioral change is really hard. Don't spend your time trying to inject qualities that may not be there. Instead focus on drawing out those inherent qualities that are already present. That in itself is a huge challenge.

It's important to remember that the job of a good leader is to draw out and enable the best in his or her people. They are not, unless they want the job, a therapist committed to long-term action. Leadership is all about results. Results in a compassionate way, results with support and heart, results with an understanding that you impact people's lives—but results nonetheless.

If you focus on bringing out what is already there versus trying to create what may not be present, you will be more effective and successful in managing your people. So the next time you have a tough management issue with an employee, consider long and hard his or her capacity to change. It may be possible. But the odds are it may not be time well spent. Instead, try a tactic that focuses quickly on the bottom line with a bias for results.

And if your gut tells you it's not working—take action. Remember, when you cut off a dog's tail, it's not less painful to the dog if you do it an inch at a time.

THE BEST WORDS ON LEADERSHIP I'VE EVER READ

It's true. The more things change, the more they stay the same. The following is by the Chinese philosopher Lao-tzu, author of the *Tao Te Ching,* or "The Way." His writing forms the basis for Taoism. Given all that has been authored on the subject, these simple words strike me as the best I have ever read about the simple truth of true leadership. This was written in the sixth century B.C.

> True leaders
> are hardly known to their followers.
> Next after them are the leaders
> the people know and admire;
> after them, are those they fear;
> after them, those they despise.

To give no trust
is to get no trust.
When the work's done right,
with no fuss or boasting,
ordinary people say,
"Oh, we did it."

THE GREATEST GIFT
OF CHANGE

**The problem with learning from experience
is we get the test before the lesson.**

—*Mad Magazine*'s Alfred E. Neuman

The greatest gift of change is what it teaches us about ourselves. Change is the university of universities when it comes to self-knowledge. And the final exams happen every day.

Every major change will severely test a leader's limits and behaviors—and the bigger the change, the bigger the test. A leader's psychological patterns—the good, the bad, and the ugly—will inevitably take center stage in an organization's life during such times. If a leader has a strong need for control, it will show; if he or she craves attention, it will become obvious. In fact, any disruptive or dysfunctional pattern—insecurity, power obsession, fear of scarcity, neediness, conflict avoidance—you name it and it will rear its ugly head.

All the world's a mirror. And when an organization's in flux, change is the biggest mirror of all.

Some leaders claim they don't allow their personal issues to affect them at work. At best, that is foolish denial. Because of the amount of time we spend at work, the chance of our personal problems getting triggered in a business setting are extremely high.

But there's good news in all of this—the fact that change provides a chance to really learn about your leadership strengths and weaknesses. If your goal is to become a better leader, you need to be better prepared for the next wave of change that hits your organization. And no education is better than the situation you're currently in.

But if you really want to learn from the laboratory of change, it requires an unwavering commitment to truth—both in how you see yourself and in the culture of honesty you are willing to promote.

Look especially for the personal patterns that show up in you when triggered by change. Universally, these patterns are rooted in three areas—fear, pride, and control.

Fear patterns are based on the leader's sense of loss. They often look like an extreme need for attention or approval, a tendency to avoid conflict, and a denial of tough issues. Pride patterns are rooted in low self-esteem and will often look like arrogance, vanity, or a desire to look good regardless. Finally, control patterns often wear the face of power struggle, reflecting a need to be right, stubbornness, and high reactivity.

Here's a suggestion. Every Friday, ask yourself, "What harmful patterns showed themselves in me at work this week? Where have I been overly prideful, control-oriented, or fearful?" Focus only on yourself. If you feel adventurous, keep a short log. Over time, try to track these patterns and how they manifest themselves in you as a leader. The goal is to be honest and judgment-free. And congratulate yourself for the effort—very few leaders even dare to ask the questions.

On a larger scale, however, a culture of honesty involves more than just self-reflection. It involves others. A great paradox of leadership is that the higher you rise in an organization, the more information you will need to make the right decisions; but the higher you rise, the less information you will be freely given, as people become increasingly intimidated by your power and prestige.

This was well understood by the early Romans, who attempted to mitigate against power's seductive qualities. For instance, when an emperor returned to Rome a conquering hero, the roads were usually filled with throngs of well-wishers and ecstatic supporters. Yet, with every Caesar a tradition was instituted to reduce the seduction of the message. A slave always rode with Caesar in his chariot. As the crowds screamed their adoration, the slave's only job was to continue to whisper, "Thou art only human, Caesar. Thou art only human, Caesar."

Having a few truth-tellers—individuals who will give you the straight truth about your effectiveness and lack thereof—is essential for leaders who want to really learn and grow from change. You need someone you trust who can say things like, "It seems that you're more concerned about looking good than about making the right decision." But be careful how you react. Business is not baseball—you don't get three strikes. The first time you move into a punitive response rather than say, "Thank you. That's new information to me," you will forfeit that person's honesty for good.

My dear friend David Knudsen is a passionate fisherman. He told me once, "You know, I've fished all over the world. The waters are always different, the fish different, the line different, the bait different. Only one thing never changes—me—the fisherman."

The only consistent factor in all the changes that occur around you is you. If you are willing to see change for the gift it truly is, you will begin to experience a sense of opportunity in even the most challenging situations. If life is not about making as much money as we can, then what is it about? From my view, it's about learning—and ultimately it's about learning and improving ourselves. In that quest, change can be our biggest ally.

ABOUT THE AUTHOR

 David Baum, Ph.D., is president of D.H. Baum & Associates, a consulting firm specializing in complex systems change. Major clients include a roster of the Who's Who of the Fortune 500, such as IBM, Eastman Kodak, Shell Oil, AT&T, and Merck & Company. He also devotes one month per year to pro bono projects, including conflict resolution in Belfast; tribal revitalization in Native American communities; and as lead consultant for President Clinton's Summit for America's Future, chaired by Colin Powell.

Baum received his master's and doctorate degrees in organizational behavior from Temple University. A sought-after speaker and lecturer, Baum captivates his audiences with an eclectic background that includes stints as a clown, fire-eater, and storyteller for various circus companies.